Schools Council
Research Studies

Special Provision
for Disturbed Pupils:
a Survey

Other books in this series

Schools Council
Research Studies

Special Provision for Disturbed Pupils: a Survey

R. L. Dawson

Macmillan Education

First published 1980

Published by
MACMILLAN EDUCATION LTD
Houndmills Basingstoke Hampshire RG 21 2XS
and London
Associated companies in Delhi Dublin
Hong Kong Johannesburg Lagos Melbourne
New York Singapore and Tokyo

Printed in Hong Kong

Contents

Appendices

Acknowledgements

A report of this nature is clearly only possible through the help and co-operation of a large number of people. I should like here to acknowledge my gratitude to everyone on the Consultative Committee, particularly the other members of the project team, for what is reported here is very much the result of a team effort.

Additionally, I should like to record my thanks to the entire staff of the Inner London Education Authority's Research and Statistics branch for the help and facilities they provided to enable the analysis of the data by computer—particularly Roger Burley and Eric Midgley, who 'de-bugged' constantly and cheerfully. I should like to thank Peter Coxhead of the Department of Educational Enquiry at the University of Aston who carried out the Wishart Cluster analysis, and those other members of that department who frequently chipped in with ideas. Transferring illegible handwritten scripts and tables into a legible typed format was basically the work of Yvonne Ashdown, supported by unknown typists hidden within Philippa Fawcett College.

Finally, my thanks to the staff of the Schools Council itself, notably Norman Williams and Murray Ward for overseeing the statistics, and to the editor of the report, a member of the Schools Council Publications Section.

Tables

Foreword

The need for a project on the curricular needs of pupils with emotional and/or behavioural difficulties arose out of discussions in the Schools Council's Working Party on Special Education. This joint working party, established in 1969, included representatives of the Council's four main steering committees, with additional members selected on the basis of their experience in working with different categories of handicapped pupils. The working party had already supported seven projects in special education by the time this project on the Education of Disturbed Pupils was approved in 1974. The project ran for three years from the beginning of September 1975 to the end of August 1978 and was based on the Philippa Fawcett College of Education in South London.

This research study is a factual account of the main findings from the questionnaires to special schools for maladjusted children and to special classes and units for disturbed and disruptive pupils.

These findings are placed in a wider context, including opinion and comment, in the final report from the project by its directors, Dr Mary Wilson and Mrs Mary Evans. *Education of Disturbed Pupils* is published as Schools Council Working Paper 65 by Evans/Methuen Educational.

Introduction

The survey reported here was part of the Schools Council Project on the Education of Disturbed Pupils. The project was set up as a result of a proposal in 1973 by Dr. Mary Wilson and Mrs. Mary Evans that the Schools Council should fund an investigation into the ways in which the curriculum could further the personal adjustment and educational progress of maladjusted pupils. During the committee stages of the proposal concern was expressed for the large number of disturbed pupils, whether formally designated as maladjusted or not, who are being educated in ordinary schools. This concern was well justified. In 1972 the total number of pupils in schools was 8 364 346, and of these only 8 952 were known to be in schools and classes for the maladjusted (DES, 1972). A number of surveys have suggested that the incidence of children with psychiatric disorder* is somewhere between six and fifteen per cent, which on the 1972 statistics would represent between 501 860 and 1 254 651 pupils. These figures clearly show that, even if an incidence rate of only one per cent were assumed, the greater proportion of children with a psychiatric disorder would be on the rolls of ordinary schools. The proposed project was consequently called the Education of Disturbed Pupils so as not to exclude from the investigation children showing signs of disturbance but not officially recognized as maladjusted.

For several reasons, however, much of the project's emphasis was to remain on the special schools for the maladjusted. In these schools, for example, the majority of the children are clearly identified as disturbed and the operating curriculum designed specifically with disturbed children in mind. Also many of these schools have been dealing with disturbed

---

* The term psychiatric disorder was used in the Isle of Wight studies and has since been used by many researchers. Basically the term was defined in the studies as an abnormality of behaviour, emotions, or relationships and sufficiently marked or sufficiently prolonged to cause handicap to the child himself and/or distress or disturbance in the family or community (Rutter *et al.*, 1970).

1

children for a considerable number of years and their staffs are therefore very likely to be in a position to know which techniques and methods for the treatment of disturbed children have stood the test of time, experience and practice.

The project commenced in September 1975 and Dr. Wilson and Mrs. Evans were appointed directors assisted by two research officers, Miss J. S. Kiek and the author. All four members of the team had previous practical experience of working with disturbed children. The aim of the project was to investigate successful practice in the educational treatment of disturbed pupils with a view to offering guidance to the many teachers in ordinary and special schools who are concerned about pupils showing evidence of emotional disturbance or deviant behaviour. To do this the project proposed to look at the curriculum interpreted in its widest sense to include attitudes and relationships, as well as educational content and methods, with more emphasis on the way pupils are treated than on the administrative arrangements or type of placement. The two main forms of data collection used were questionnaires and also one-day interview and observation visits and longer visits to selected schools. Three questionnaires were constructed and sent as appropriate to:

1 (QA) All special schools for the maladjusted appearing on DES lists 42 (1974) and 70 (1974);
2 (QB) Selected schools other than special schools for the maladjusted;
3 (QC) Special classes, autonomous units and attached units primarily for disturbed pupils.*

It is with the first of these questionnaires, the questionnaire to schools for the maladjusted, that this report is primarily concerned although reference to the other two questionnaires, particularly that to classes and units, will be made where thought necessary or appropriate.

At the commencement of the project there had been no survey or report concerning schools for the maladjusted at a national level since the *Report of the Committee on Maladjusted Children* (The Underwood Report) some twenty years before. During this long period it was known that the number of schools for the maladjusted had increased about four-fold and it was thought that many changes in the thinking and practice of the schools might have also taken place. The main aim of the questionnaire therefore was to build up a comprehensive picture of both current practice in special schools for the maladjusted and the body of knowledge and opinion regarding the overall treatment of the maladjusted possessed by the staffs of these schools.

---

* For details of schools, special classes and units selection and response rate see Appendix A

THE QUESTIONNAIRE TO SPECIAL SCHOOLS

The questionnaire was a long and detailed document with forty-seven diverse question areas regarding: the schools, staff, pupils, supporting agencies, the care and control of pupils, the educational programme and teaching methods, medical and psychological treatments, work with families, methods of recording and assessment, and factors impeding the work of the schools (see Appendix B). Despite the length and complexity of the questionnaire, the team were confident of a good response since staff in these schools are generally known to be highly motivated in their work and anxious that it should be recognized nationally. The project team developed the questionnaire carefully, and often painfully, working from their own knowledge and experience of schools for the maladjusted, reviewing the available literature, and exchanging views with experienced teachers of the maladjusted, many of whom were taking advanced diploma or degree courses in the education of maladjusted children.

A pilot questionnaire was sent to ten schools randomly selected from the schools for the maladjusted appearing on the DES lists 42 (1974) and 70 (1974). As a result of this pilot survey and the comments of the teachers consulted some small amendments were made to the questionnaire but insufficient to merit a second pilot, particularly in view of the time scale of the project and the already small total population of schools. The final version of the questionnaire was sent to the remaining 178 listed schools, six of which were later found to be inappropriate for inclusion in the sample (172 schools). A total of 114 appropriate schools returned the question-naire (66 %). Fourteen schools reported that there were reasons why they could not complete the questionnaire and nine questionnaires were reported as lost in transit. Subsequent to sending the questionnaire, contact was thus made with 137 schools (80 %). The relative distributions among the responding schools of maintained schools and schools not maintained and administered by a local education authority, and boarding, mixed day/boarding and day schools—apart from a slight under-representation of day schools—compared adequately with the estimated distribution of these schools among the total number (see Chapter 1).

Response to the questionnaire was generally highly favourable, to give but two examples, 'a most excellent document' and 'a magnificently searching questionnaire'. Many asked to have copies of the questionnaire to continue 'the useful and valuable staff discussions' it had promoted and many commented on its complexity and the difficulty they had found in completing it but, with one exception, this was seen as a meritorious feature. The one exception wrote, 'This questionnaire is in my opinion too complex to be of real value. Less detail would produce a more realistic appraisal. It was like completing *The Times* crossword'. Those respondents reading this report may find some consolation in knowing that the complexities and difficulties experienced by the research team in analysing the questionnaire were probably no less than they had themselves experienced in completing it.

THE ANALYSIS

Nearly one half of all the questions were open-ended in that respondents were able to give free answer to those questions. The difficulties of analysis associated with the use of open-ended questions are well known and were known to the team during the construction of the questionnaire. The high proportion of open-ended questions is a reflection, firstly, of the lack of information about many of the areas of current practice and opinion in the schools and, secondly, of the team's reluctance to impose preconceived structures upon such areas. To be able to deal with the large number of variables covered by the questionnaire, a lot of the data was coded for computer processing. For most of the questions this was simply a matter of transcribing responses from the questionnaire to a coding booklet. For most of the open-ended questions it was found possible to evolve an appropriate coding frame. The bulk of the data analysis was carried out through use of the *Statistical Package for the Social Sciences* (Nie et al, 1970).

As certain variables, for example the age range of pupils catered for by a school, could be expected to influence or determine to some extent the operating curriculum, the data were systematically explored on the following independent variables: maintaining authority of school (LEA maintained or not-maintained, although, as there were no 'not maintained' day schools in the sample, comparisons between maintained and not-maintained schools refer to boarding schools only); school type (day, boarding or mixed day/boarding schools); age range of pupils (junior, middle, senior or all-age schools), and number of years open as a school for maladjusted children (seven years or less, eight to twelve years, thirteen years or more). As will be seen in Chapter 1, although there was an insufficient number of girls' schools to permit valid comparisons with boys' schools, data relating only to girls' schools were examined along certain major variables. For the specified independent variables only statistically significant differences along any dependent variable will be commented upon; for all other dependent variables a case of no significant difference can be assumed.

Unless otherwise specified the statistical tests and measures of correlation used throughout were, according to the level of measurement incorporated in the data: chi-squared; analysis of variance; Spearman rank correlation coefficients (ρ); Pearson product-moment correlation coefficient (*r*). Two-tail tests of significance were used for both correlation coefficients.

PURPOSE OF THE REPORT

The main purpose of this report is to make easily available to other interested workers in this field as much of the statistical data accruing from analysis of the questionnaire to schools for the maladjusted as is reasonable. As no doubt the reader is well aware from the length and complexity of this questionnaire the amount of data is enormous, and naturally some selection has had to be made. Presenting such a large amount of data obviously requires also a certain degree of structuring by the presenter. The structure adopted can be quite clearly seen from the chapter headings, but it is recognized that a quite different structure could be equally valid. The various chapters should not be viewed as exclusive; for example, although Chapter 4 is called the Treatment Programme and Chapter 5 is called the Educational Programme, it is recognized that the educational programme cannot operate in a vacuum and is regarded in almost every school as an integral and essential part of the overall treatment programme.

In order to make available as much of the data as possible within the constraints mentioned, detailed discussion of findings, references to other relevant research, and possible implications for future practice or research will be kept to a minimum and, where they occur, be brief.

The placing of the data in a wider context and consideration of the possible implications will be an integral part of the final report of the full project (Wilson and Evans, 1980), due for presentation to the Schools Council early in 1979. Another purpose of this report is to free the project's final report from the necessity of presenting detailed statistical data within the text to support its conclusions.

Finally, it is hoped that this report will help to revitalize, and contribute to, the discussions raised by the questionnaire and possibly prompt other research in this area of growing importance.

1 The special schools, units and classes

THE SPECIAL SCHOOLS

The data reported in this section are concerned only with those 114 schools for the maladjusted in England and Wales that returned a completed questionnaire. A detailed numerical breakdown of the total provision of special schools for the maladjusted compiled from DES statistics, is available in concise form in *Educating Maladjusted Children* (Laslett, 1977).

Only one quarter (25 %) of the responding schools operate without some residential provision, that is accepting pupils only on a daily attendance basis. Over a half (58 %) accept pupils only on a boarding basis, while the remaining 17 % accept pupils both on a boarding and a daily basis, though in such schools boarding pupils greatly outnumber day pupils.

Seventy per cent of the schools are maintained and administered by Local Education Authorities (LEAs), the remainder being maintained and administered by private individuals or registered charities or trusts. With one exception all of the not-maintained schools accept pupils only on a residential basis, the one exception taking both day and boarding pupils. Schools in the not-maintained sector play a substantial part in the overall provision of special schools for the maladjusted in England and Wales, particularly in the provision of boarding schools and among our responding schools the not-maintained sector contributes 48 % of boarding schools. More than one third (36 %) of the schools are 'all-age schools', catering for pupils across the whole school age range; 15 % are 'junior schools', catering only for pupils below the age of twelve years, and 45 % are 'senior schools', catering only for pupils above ten years of age. The few remaining schools are 'middle schools', catering only for pupils between the ages of eight and fourteen years; for most purposes of analysis these are combined with the junior schools. Nearly one half (48 %) of the all-age schools are day schools and 71 % of senior schools are boarding schools. Reversing this breakdown, 68 % of day schools are all-age schools, only 16 % of the boarding schools are primary schools while 55 % are senior

6

schools. Of the not-maintained schools 55 % are senior schools and 23 % primary, and, of the LEA schools, 42 % are senior and 17 % primary. Table 1.1 summarizes the data from this and the preceding paragraph by number of schools.

The mean number of pupils in the schools is 42 (median = 43), the greater proportion of schools having between 30 and 55 pupils (the largest school has 94 pupils and the smallest 12).

Junior schools are significantly smaller than senior schools ($p = 0.006$), the means being 32 for junior schools and 43 for senior schools; senior schools tend to be smaller than all-age schools, the means being 43 and 48 respectively although this difference is not statistically significant.

Within the schools boys greatly outnumber the girls, the ratio being in the order of five boys for every girl and, while just over one half (53 %) of the schools cater only for boys, less than one tenth (8 %) cater for girls only. (That behaviour problems are more prevalent among boys than girls is a well established fact. For a brief discussion of possible explanations and other reading see Rutter (1975) p. 103, and Wolff (1969) p. 201.)

Table 1.1 Type, age range and maintaining authority of schools

Type of school	Age range All-age	Junior	Senior	No Response	TOTALS
Boarding (66)					
LEA maintained	10	4	19	1	34
Not-maintained	7	7	17	1	32
Day (28)					
LEA maintained	19	8	1	—	28
Not-maintained	—	—	—	—	—
Mixed boarding/ day (19)					
LEA maintained	3	1	14	—	18
Not-maintained	—	1	—	—	1
				TOTAL	113*

*One all-age school failed to specify type or maintaining authority

The overall pupil-to-teacher ratio for the schools is one full-time teacher to every 6/7 pupils. This means that the great proportion of schools, having between 30 and 55 pupils, will have a full-time teaching staff of between 5 and 8 teachers, including the headteacher. Most of the schools do not have part-time teachers but, of those which do, nearly one half have more than one. LEA schools have a lower pupil to full-time teacher ratio (6·2:1) than the not-maintained schools (8·3:1), although these schools tend to have a lower pupil to part-time teacher ratio of 21:1 as compared to 58:1. Day schools tend to have a lower pupil to full-time teacher ratio than boarding schools (5·4:1 and 6·8:1) but the respective part-time ratios are very similar. Regarding the age range catered for by a school, primary schools have a lower full-time ratio (5·9:1) than senior schools (6·9:1), the part-time ratios being quite similar.

Boarding schools have one full-time child care worker for every 7 or 8 pupils which means that the typical boarding school will have a full-time child care staff of around six. Over one third of these schools will also have up to three part-time child care workers. Nearly all the day schools have at least one child care worker, the majority (86 %) having a full-time worker. As with the teaching staff, maintained schools tend to have slightly more full-time care staff than those not maintained but the latter make more use of part-time care staff than do the former.

SPECIAL CLASSES AND UNITS

A total of 173 completed questionnaires for special classes and units (C/Us) (see Appendix C) were returned. Thirteen respondents failed to specify either whether they are administratively part of a parent school or autonomous or if they cater only for pupils from the parent school or from a number of schools. Of the remaining 160 C/Us, 38 % indicated that they were autonomous and cater for pupils from more than one school (autonomous units); 36 % indicated that they are administratively part of a parent school but accept pupils from a number of schools (attached units); and the remaining 26 % specified that they are administratively part of a parent school and accept only pupils from that school (special classes).

Of the total respondents, 43 % are for pupils under the age of 12 (junior C/Us), 4 % are for pupils between the ages of 8 and 14 years (middle C/Us), 39 % are for pupils above the age of 10 years (senior C/Us) and 14 % are for pupils of all ages. The number of C/Us broken down by type and age range is shown in Table 1.2. This table shows that over three-quarters of the

Table 1.2   Type of special class or unit and age range ($n = 160$)

Type	Age range All-age	Junior	Middle	Senior	TOTALS
Autonomous units	20	17	4	20	61
Attached units	1	44	2	10	57
Special classes	0	10	0	32	42

special classes are for senior-age pupils only and that a similar proportion of the attached units are for junior-age children. Autonomous units are almost equally likely to be for junior-age pupils only, for senior-age pupils only, or for pupils of all ages. All-age provision is almost exclusively by the autonomous unit, a little over one half of the senior-age provision is by special class and well over one half of the junior-age provision is by attached unit.

Just over one half (53 %) of the special classes and units accept pupils on a full-time attendance basis only, 17 % accept pupils on a part-time attendance basis only and 27 % accept both full-time and part-time pupils. (3 % could not be identified in this way.) This mixture of part-time and full-time attendance makes it difficult to give simple statistics for the number of pupils attending a special class or unit. The most useful information in this respect accrues from the data relating to the minimum and maximum number of pupils attending at any one time and is shown in Table 1.3 (The greatest maximum number of pupils attending a special class or unit at any one time is 65.) More than one half of special classes (62 %) and autonomous units (51 %) accept some pupils on a part-time basis but only slightly over a quarter (26 %) of attached units do so. Conversely, while 98 % of attached units accept pupils on a full-time attendance basis, only 74 % of autonomous units and 60 % of classes do so. Slightly over one half of all-age and senior-age C/Us accept pupils on a part-time basis (56 % and 52 % respectively), but only 28 % of junior-age C/Us do so. Ninety-one per cent of junior-age, 78 % of senior-age and 64 % of all-age C/Us accept full-time attending pupils.

Table 1.3 Minimum and maximum numbers of pupils attending special classes and units

Type of C/U	Minimum		Maximum	
	Mean	Median	Mean	Median
Autonomous unit	13	10	17	14
Attached unit	9	7	13	10
Special class	7	5	12	9
All classes and units	10	7	14	12

The type and age range of C/Us broken down by full-time, part-time or both full- and part-attendance is shown in Table 1.4. The table shows that nearly three-quarters of all attached units and all junior age range C/Us cater for full-time attending pupils only but the strong relationship between attached units and junior-age-range C/Us shown in Table 1.2 should be noted when considering these data. It seems reasonable to assume,

Table 1.4   Type and age range of special classes and units broken down by proportion of time attended

Class or unit	Full time	Part time	Full time/ Part time
Type			
Autonomous unit	29	15	16
Attached unit	42	1	14
Special class	12	13	13
Age range			
Junior	53	7	14
Middle	0	4	3
Senior	28	11	24
All age	10	8	6

however, that it is the nature of the attached unit, rather than the age range catered for, that is the major factor in accounting for this finding.

The large majority of classes and units cater for both boys and girls, the population of boys being about twice as large as that for girls. Autonomous and attached units have more than twice as many boys than girls but in the special classes, while there are still more boys than girls, the proportions are not so different. Junior-age classes and units have more than three times as many boys as girls but there are less than twice as many boys as girls in senior-age classes and units. As most of the junior-age provision is in the attached units, and as much of the senior-age provision is in the special classes, the differences in sex distribution between the classes and units and between those catering for different age ranges cannot be explained simply.

Most classes and units have only full-time teaching staff, 90% having only one or two full-time teachers (mean 1·9, median 1·4). The mean for the autonomous units is 2·5, which compares to 1·5 for both the special classes and the attached units. From the numbers of pupils attending the different types of provision, the pupil to teacher ratio is around 6:1 for the autonomous units and around 7–8:1 for the classes and attached units.

Over one half of both types of unit had one or two other than teaching full-time staff, whereas less than 10% of classes have such assistance.

Question 5 of the questionnaire to special classes and units asked recipients to indicate, using three pre-specified categories, the main purpose of the class or unit. Table 1.5 shows the responses to this question and the first three categories in the table are those specified in the question.

It can be seen that nearly 90% of the classes and units see *giving emotional/social help* as at least part of their main purpose while less than

Table 1.5   Purpose of classes or units

Purpose	No. C/Us	%
1 To help pupils with emotional/social problems	85	49
2 To give educational help	14	8
3 To relieve other classes or schools	1	1
Both 1 and 2	45	26
Both 1 and 3	5	3
Both 2 and 3	1	1
1, 2 and 3	19	11
Not stated	3	2

50 % see *educational help* either solely as or part of their main purpose and only 16 % see part or all of their main purpose as *relieving other schools or classes*. The different types of provision tend to view their purpose similarly, although special classes—much more than the units—see part of their purpose as *to relieve other classes*.

SUMMARY

Special schools for the maladjusted are extremely small by the standards of ordinary schools, most operating on a residential basis; only one quarter operate on the basis of daily attendance only. There are some interesting similarities and differences between special school and non-special school provision for disturbed pupils. In both categories of provision pupil-teacher ratios are much lower than those found in ordinary schools where the ratios are around 24:1 for primary schools and 17:1 for senior schools. In the special schools boys outnumber girls by about 5 to 1 but in the special classes and units they do so by only around 2 to 1. Only 15 % of special schools cater exclusively for pupils below the age of twelve years, whereas some 43 % of special classes and units do so. The proportions catering exclusively for senior age pupils are somewhat similar but, while 35 % of the special schools cater for pupils of all ages, only 14 % of the special classes and units do so.

2 The pupils

The fact that a child has been diagnosed as maladjusted and/or is attending a school for maladjusted tells one little about his specific behavioural or emotional problems or their severity. *The Handicapped Pupils and School Health Service Regulations* (Ministry of Education, 1945) define maladjusted pupils as 'those who show evidence of emotional instability or psychological disturbance and require special educational treatment in order to effect their personal, social or educational readjustment'. The purpose of this definition in the regulations was not to provide any exact criteria for identifying maladjusted children but rather to make it legally possible for special educational facilities to be provided for them. In practice the term 'maladjustment' encompasses a whole range of very different behavioural and emotional problems and, in order to establish the sort of problems the schools for the maladjusted were dealing with, it was necessary to break the term down into a number of categories. The categorization adopted for the survey was based upon a pupil's predominant pattern of behaviour and was developed from the diagnostic categories used in the Isle of Wight studies (Rutter et al., 1970), the principal departures being as follows:

a) the 'hyperkinetic syndrome' category was omitted
b) a category 'neurological abnormalities' was added
c) a category 'educational difficulties' was added.

A brief description of the behaviours to be included within each category was given and the full categorization and descriptions used appear in question 9 of the questionnaire to special schools (see Appendix B).

Although the project team was concerned that many schools might be reluctant to classify their children according to their predominant patterns of behaviour, of the 114 responding schools, 106 (93 %) completed the question. Furthermore, as can be seen in Table 2.1, of those responding, the vast majority felt able to fit all, or almost all, of their children into the specified categories.

Table 2.1 shows that pupils with behaviour symptomatic of a conduct disorder form the largest single group and, if we include the percentage who manifest such behaviour in conjunction with that of a neurotic disorder, no fewer than 58 % of pupils in schools for the maladjusted display elements of the behaviour patterns associated with conduct disorders (that is, socially unacceptable behaviour such as aggression, destructiveness, stealing, lying, truanting and so on).

Table 2.1   Predominant patterns of behaviour of pupils in special schools (Q9)

n*	Predominant pattern of behaviour	Mean %	Median %
95	Conduct disorders	40	38
99	Neurotic disorders	18	13
91	Mixed conduct/neurotic disorders	18	13
71	Developmental disorders	9	6
54	Psychosis	3	2
58	Personality disorders	4	2
58	Neurological disorders	4	2
48	Educational disorders	4	0
12	Other disorders	1	0

* 106 schools responded to this question. n refers to the number of schools indicating that a percentage of their pupils are described by the particular pattern of behaviour.

The table also shows that 18 % of pupils display symptoms associated with neurotic disorder, such as excessive anxiety, depression, isolation, phobia, tics, and that a further 18 % show these symptoms in conjunction with those of conduct disorder. In total, the three groups of *conduct disorders*, *neurotic disorders*, and *mixed conduct/neurotic disorders* make up 76 % of all pupils in these schools. Only five schools felt unable to place some of their pupils in at least two of these three groups and two of the five placed more than 90 % of their pupils in the mixed conduct/neurotic group.

The predominance of the three groups of conduct, neurotic and mixed conduct/neurotic disorders resembles the findings of other surveys.

Of the children diagnosed as having a psychiatric disorder in the Isle of Wight studies 34 % were placed in the conduct disorder group, 34 % in the neurotic group and 21 % in the mixed group, that is a total of nearly 90 % in these three groups alone (Rutter et al., 1970). In a study of admissions to a child psychiatric clinic over a three-year period Phillip Barker reported that 65 % of the children admitted came within these three groups (Barker, 1974). It is not surprising that the prevalence of these groups in the current survey more closely resembles Barker's selected clinical group than the Isle of Wight study which was based on a total age group.

The fourth largest group is that described by the *developmental disorder* category but, as for all of the remaining groups, the distribution is far from normal. Thirty-one schools reported that they had no children who were adequately described by this category and, although only thirteen reported that they had 10 % or more, five put 40 % or more in this group. Fifty-two schools reported that they had no *psychotic* children and only seven reported that they had 10 % or more. For both *personality disorders* 'and *neurological disorders* forty-eight schools reported none with only twelve reporting 10 % or above for personality disorders and only eleven for neurological disorders. For *educational disorders* fifty-eight schools reported none but fifteen reported 10 % or more. Only twelve schools placed a percentage of their children in the *other disorders* category and only three of these gave estimates of 10 % or more. The skewed distributions of some of these less common disorders may be due to variations in interpretation of the different categories rather than actual differences in the populations of the schools.

No significant differences in the distributions of the disorders were found between the day and boarding schools; the LEA schools and the not-maintained schools, and the newly established and the long established schools. Some notable differences were found for certain disorders between schools catering for different age ranges. These are shown in Table 2.2. For *neurological disorder* the difference between the junior and senior schools is highly significant ($p < 0.004$) and, while the differences between these schools for the other three groups of disorder in the table do not attain the traditional minimum 5 % level of significance, they are all at or very near the 10 % level. As the means for the all-age schools, with the exception of *personality disorder*, tend to fall between those for the junior and senior schools the results offer the suggestion that the incidence of neurological disorders, personality disorders and childhood *psychosis* tend to decrease

Table 2.2   Predominant patterns of behaviour of pupils by age range of schools (in percentages)

Behaviour pattern	Junior mean $n = 16$	Senior mean $n = 50$	All age mean $n = 35$
Psychosis	4·6	2·1	3·5
Personality disorder	8·8	3·1	3·1
Neurological disorder	8·1	1·6:	4·7
Educational disorder	1·9	5·0	4·1

with age while the incidence of *educational disorders* tends to increase with age. However, it may be that these disorders are more easily and quickly recognized and consequently allocated special education in the junior age range and later, while they may not decrease numerically, they decrease proportionately as pupils with other disorders are admitted to senior-age schools. (Senior schools, it may be recalled, are larger and more numerous than junior schools.) There is also a suggestion (see Chapter 6) that children with these disorders are transferred to other placements more frequently than those exhibiting other disorders.

In the nine all-girl schools the means for the conduct disorders, neurotic disorders and mixed conduct/neurotic disorders were, in each case, around 5 % more than those for the whole sample used. Other studies (Davie, 1968 and Rutter et al., 1970) have found that in the general population girls are more likely than boys to display behaviour symptomatic of neurotic disorder and less likely to display the behaviours of conduct disorder. The results of the current study therefore suggest that girls who come within the conduct disorder category are far more likely to be admitted to special schools for the maladjusted than those who come within the neurotic disorder group. The means for the remaining categories for these all-girl schools are in every instance under one half of those for the whole sample and, in the case of educational disorders, the mean is less than one quarter of that of the total population.

The questionnaire to special classes and units asked respondents to classify their pupils into only three groups that basically coincide with the *conduct, neurotic* and *mixed conduct/neurotic* disorders of the questionnaire to special schools. Table 2.3 shows the categories used and the means and median estimates for the total number of special classes and units responding to the question. The proportional distribution for these three

Table 2.3 Predominant patterns of behaviour of pupils in special classes and units

No. of C/Us (n = 166)	Pattern of behaviour	Mean %	Median %
158	Mainly outgoing, active, aggressive, disruptive, quarrelsome, etc.	43	40
147	Mainly inward-looking, passive, anxious, fearful, socially isolated, etc.	25	25
138	With some features from both of the above groups, neither pattern predominant	26	25

categories is quite similar to that for the conduct, neurotic and mixed disorder groups of the special schools. In the classes and units, as in the special schools, it is the outgoing pattern of behaviour that is most prevalent. Only eight C/Us (5%) estimated that none of their pupils came within the outgoing group while twenty-six (16%) estimated that 75% or more came within the group, six of these estimating that all of their pupils did so. For the inward-looking group, only two estimated 75% or more. The results also suggest that there is a small proportion of children in special classes and units (6%) whose predominant pattern of behaviour is regarded by their teachers as not being adequately described by the three specified patterns.

PUPILS' IQ

Table 2.4   Distribution of pupils' IQ in special schools
(Q7)

Mean %	Median %	IQ range	
2·0	0·1	Very much above average	(above 130)
7·0	3·0	Above average	(115–129)
29·0	25·0	Average (high)	(100–114)
43·0	43·0	Average (low)	(85–99)
17·0	12·0	Below average	(70–84)
2·0	0·2	Very much below average	(below 70)

Table 2.4 shows the mean and median percentages of pupils estimated as falling within the six standard deviations of IQ. The results show that, as a group, schools for the maladjusted have more pupils in the lower half IQ ranges than one would expect to find in the normal school population. As it is generally thought however that maladjusted children under-function to some degree in test situations, and in so far as the estimates were based upon IQ test results, the actual distribution may be closer to normal than that shown in the table. The discrepancies between the means and medians in the extreme ranges show that pupils within these ranges tend to be concentrated within a few schools although no school estimated more than 50% of its pupils to be in either of the two extreme ranges.

Day schools have significantly more pupils in the very much below average and below average ranges than do the boarding schools ($p < 0.004$ and 0.005), while the boarding schools have significantly more pupils than the day schools in the average (high) range ($p < 0.003$). Primary schools have significantly more pupils in the very much below average range than do the senior or all-age schools ($p < 0.004$ and 0.05) and have more pupils in

Table 2.5 Mean percentage of pupils' IQ ranges by school type, age range and years open

IQ range	Schools Day (n = 27)	Boarding (n = 64)	Primary (n = 21)	Senior (n = 51)	All-age (n = 38)	Established 7− yrs	7+ yrs
Average (high)	19·4	32·1					
Below average	24·1	13·4	22·1	14·4	17·2		
Very much below average	5·4	0·9	6·0	0·6	1·8	4·5	0·3

the below average range also although the differences are not significant. Schools established for less than seven years have significantly more pupils in the very much below average range than those established for more than seven years ($p < 0.05$). Table 2.5 shows these data. Maintained schools have slightly more pupils in each of the three lower IQ ranges and conversely fewer in each of the higher ranges than do not-maintained schools but none of the differences attain significance.

PUPILS' ACHIEVEMENT LEVELS

Table 2.6 Pupil achievement levels on entry in relation to potential (Q8)

Achievement level	Mean %	Median %
Not underachieving	8	2
Slightly underachieving	28	25
Seriously underachieving	41	40
Very seriously underachieving	22	18

Table 2.6 shows the mean and median estimates in percentages of pupils' achievement levels on entry to the schools in relation to their potential. As no specific criteria were laid down in the questionnaire as to how to determine the degree of underachievement, only a 'not underachieving/underachieving' dichotomy can claim any objective validity and the estimates of the degree of unaderachivement are best viewed as the school's perceptions of their pupils' achievement levels. The table shows that the schools as a group estimate that 92 % of their pupils are underachieving to some extent and perceive some 63 % to be either seriously or very seriously underachieving. The quite large discrepancy between the mean and median

estimates for the not underachieving group is explained to some extent by the finding that, while some 49 schools (45 % of the 110 schools responding to this question) reported that none of their pupils had entered the school without some degree of underachievement, 8 schools reported that 25 % or more of their pupils were not underachieving on entry.

With over 92 % of pupils estimated as underachieving on entry to the schools and 64 % seen as seriously or very seriously underachieving, it is not surprising to find that 68 % of pupils are esimated as needing remedial education in the basic skills. (As might be expected, a highly significant negative correlation ($r = -0.38$, $p<0.001$) was found between the percentage of pupils estimated as not underachieving on entry and the percentage estimated as in need of remedial education.) One half of the schools estimated that 75 % or more of their pupils need remedial help, 14 % of the schools estimating that all of their pupils need such help and 38 % estimating 90 % or above. Only 3 % of the schools responded that none of their pupils require remedial help and only 7 % estimated that 15 % or less of their pupils need such help.

Day schools estimate that, on entry, fewer of their pupils are not underachieving (5 %) and perceive significantly more as very seriously underachieving (29 %) than do boarding schools (9 %, not significant, and 18 %, $p<0.03$). Primary schools perceive significantly more of their pupils as very seriously underachieving than do senior schools (37 % and 17 % respectively, $p<0.002$). Finally, maintained schools see significantly more of their pupils as seriously underachieving than do not-maintained schools (46 % and 37 % respectively, $p<0.05$).

Day schools estimate more of their pupils require remedial help than do boarding schools (73 % and 63 % respectively) and primary schools estimate more than do senior schools (75 % and 60 % respectively), although in both cases the difference does not attain significance. These differences are very much in line with the data relating to pupil achievement levels.

The IQ distribution of pupils of the nine all-girl schools does not differ fundamentally from that for the total population. These schools, however, estimate more pupils as not underachieving (mean 13 %, median 15 %) and perceive fewer as very seriously underachieving (mean 14 %, median 12 %) than do the total number of schools.

PREDOMINANT PATTERNS OF BEHAVIOUR, IQ AND ACHIEVEMENT LEVELS

The discovery of any relationships between the predominant patterns of behaviour, IQ and achievement levels of maladjusted pupils would clearly be of interest to workers in this field, and consequently the data were explored in this way. However, what is involved here must be made clear.

Schools were required to estimate the percentages of their pupils within each of the categories used in these three areas and it is these percentages that were tested for relationships and not intra-individual relationships. Significant correlation coefficients in these areas might be suggestive of intra-individual relationships but they do not validly support such relationships. Finally, because of the small percentage of pupils in the disorder categories other than the *conduct, neurotic* and *mixed conduct/neurotic*, only the significant correlations relating to these three groups will be reported.

A significant positive correlation was found between the percentage of conduct disorders within a school and the percentage of pupils in the average (low) IQ range ($r = 0.21$, $p = <0.05$, $n = 106$) and correspondingly a significant negative correlation between the percentage of conduct disorders and the percentage of pupils in the above average IQ range ($r = -0.23$, $p<0.05$). A converse trend was found for the *neurotic* disorder category. For this group there was a significant negative correlation with the very much below average IQ range ($r = -0.19$, $p<0.05$, $n = 106$) and below average IQ range ($r = -0.19$, $p<0.05$) and a significant positive correlation with the above average IQ range ($r = 0.24$, $p<0.01$). No significant correlations were found for the percentage of *mixed conduct*/neurotic disorder pupils within a school and the percentage of pupils in the various IQ ranges or achievement categories used.

There were no significant correlations between the percentage of pupils in any predominant pattern of behaviour category and the percentage of pupils estimated as being in need of remedial education.

A number of significant correlations were found between the percentage of pupils in the various IQ and achievement categories used. These are shown, together with the direction of the remaining coefficients, in Table 2.7. The matrix tends to suggest that the schools may not have closely referred to pupil potential, as specified in the question, in assessing pupil levels of achievement. These schools do have access to the full psychological assessment of their pupils made prior to entry and it can be reasonably assumed that the estimates of the percentage of pupils within the specified IQ ranges were made in reference to the measured IQs of pupils. Pupils within the very much below average IQ range could be expected to be greatly underachieving in reference to their potential, indeed very serious underachievement in relation to potential for such pupils would perhaps represent no achievement whatsoever.

The matrix, however, shows the percentage of pupils in the very much below average IQ range to be positively, and highly significantly correlated with the percentage of pupils estimated as very seriously underachieving according to potential and to be negatively correlated with the other specified achievement levels. The remaining coefficients are open to

Table 2.7   Correlation coefficients and levels of significance between pupils' IQ ranges and levels of achievement ($n = 109$)

IQ range related to average	Degree of underachievement None	Slight	Serious	Very serious
Very much above	—	+	—	—
Above	+	+ 0·26**	—	—
Average (high)	+ 0·19*	+ 0·37***	—	− 0·36***
Average (low)	—	− 0·22*	+ 0·26**	—
Below	—	—	—	+ 0·21*
Very much below	—	− 0·20*	—	+ 0·35***

  * $p \leqslant 0.05$
 ** $p \leqslant 0.01$
*** $p \leqslant 0.001$

somewhat similar reasoning. The tentative quality of the suggestion needs to be reiterated and is further underlined by recalling the caveat given at the beginning of this section that none of the relationships explored here necessarily refer to intra-individual relationships.

PUPILS' EDUCATIONAL PROBLEMS IN SPECIAL CLASSES AND UNITS

As it was known that some special classes and units do not have access to a measured IQ for all of their pupils, the IQ of pupils was not explored in the questionnaire to classes and units. Achievement levels as such were not explored either but the classes and units were asked to estimate what percentage of their pupils had special educational problems, and these results are shown in Table 2.8.

Table 2.8   Educational problems of pupils attending special classes or units ($n = 163$)

Educational problem	Mean (%)	Median (%)
(a) No educational problem	11	4
(b) Some retardation in general school work	19	10
(c) Need remedial help in the basic subjects	23	9
(d) Both (b) and (c)	47	33

It is interesting to note that a total of 66 % of pupils show some retardation in general school work and some 70 % need remedial help in the basic subjects. The quite large discrepancy between the mean and median percentages for pupils with no educational problem is largely explained by the finding that 78 classes or units (48 %) estimated that none of their pupils came within this category while 8 (5 %) reported that 50 % or more did so. The other discrepancies between mean and median estimates can be similarly explained. Seventy-five (46 %) reported that they had no pupils with *some retardation*, but 20 (12 %) reported 50 % or more, 2 of these reporting 100 %. Seventy-eight (48 %) reported no pupils as *needing remedial help* but 33 (18 %) reported 50 % or more, 13 of these reporting 100 %. Finally, 44 (27 %) reported no pupils with both *some retardation* and *needing remedial help*, while 72 (42 %) reported 50 % or more with 37 of these reporting 100 %.

The findings for the educational problems of pupils broken down by type and age range of special class or unit are shown in Table 2.9. Because no specific criteria were given for the separate categories only a *no special problems/some problems* dichotomy can lay claim to objective validity and the differences shown in Table 2.9 therefore may result from differences in teacher perceptions rather than in pupils' actual problems.

Table 2.9   Educational problems of pupils by type and age range of special class or unit (in percentages)

(i) Problem	Type of C/U		
	Classes ($n = 38$)	Attached units ($n = 55$)	Autonomous units ($n = 57$)
(a) No special problems	12	10	13
(b) Some retardation**	30	13	17
(c) Need for remedial help	26	23	23
(d) Both (b) and (c)*	32	54	47

(ii) Problem	Age range of C/U		
	Junior ($n = 72$)	Senior ($n = 62$)	All age ($n = 22$)
(a) No special problems	10	11	17
(b) Some retardation**	11	27	19
(c) Need for remedial help	26	23	15
(d) Both (b) and (c)	53	38	49

* $p \leqslant 0.05$
** $p \leqslant 0.01$

PUPILS IN ORDINARY SCHOOLS

As emphasized in Appendix A, ordinary school respondents to the questionnaire to schools other than those for the maladjusted cannot be regarded as a representative sample of ordinary schools. There are, nevertheless, some interesting data from these schools capable of generating useful and testable hypotheses.

Table 2.10 Estimated   ranges   of   pupils'
intelligence ($n = 141$)

Level of intelligence	Mean %	Median %
Above average	20	20
Average intelligence	50	50
Below average	30	30

The estimated ranges of pupils' intelligence (shown in Table 2.10) approximates, apart from slightly more in the below average range, to those one would expect in the general population. The mean percentage of pupils estimated as showing significant disturbance of behaviour and/or emotion was 12%, (median 10%). The correlation coefficients computed for the percentage of pupils within the three intelligence ranges and the percentage estimated as disturbed were all significant as follows: percentage of pupils disturbed and percentage of pupils of below average intelligence, $r = 0.42$ ($p<0.001$); percentage of pupils disturbed and percentage of pupils of average intelligence, $r = 0.17$ ($p<0.05$); percentage of pupils disturbed and percentage of pupils of above average intelligence $r = -0.33$ ($p<0.001$). These results show that the more pupils a school estimates as being below average in intelligence, the greater the percentage of its pupils it is likely to estimate as *disturbed*. Clearly the converse also holds in that the greater percentage of pupils a school estimates as being above average in intelligence, the smaller the percentage of pupils it will be likely to perceive as disturbed. This is not to be taken to imply that low intelligence 'causes' disturbance (evidence from the range of intelligence within the special schools refutes this), nor is it necessarily the case that the respective percentages refer to the same groups of children. The data refer to school populations and not to individual pupils or specific groups of pupils. Finally as no standardized criteria were given for either variable, it is best to view the results in terms of how schools perceive pupils rather than as objective measures.

The correlation coefficient was also computed for the number of pupils attending a school and the percentage estimated as showing signs of disturbance. Although the coefficient did not attain significance, $r = -0.15$, $p < 0.08$, that it has a negative sign is of interest. The suggestion is that the greater the number of pupils attending a school, the smaller the percentage of pupils estimated as showing signs of disturbance. The reader is left to ponder upon the numerous possible explanations.

SUMMARY

The majority of pupils in both special schools for the maladjusted and in other special provisions for disturbed children are likely to be reported showing behaviour that is outgoing and active rather than behaviour that is inward-looking and passive. While the distribution of pupils' intelligence in both forms of provision may be very nearly normal there are few pupils within the special schools who are considered to be not under-achieving according to their potential on entry, and in the schools at any one time a majority are thought to require specific remedial help in the basic subjects. Similarly, in the special classes and units for the disturbed, few pupils are considered to be without educational problems and the majority are thought to require remedial help in the basic subjects.

3 The staff

It will be remembered from Chapter 1 that, in general, special schools have one full-time teacher to every 6 or 7 pupils and that special classes and units also have much lower pupil-teacher ratios than do ordinary schools. Such pupil-teacher ratios obviously facilitate a high level of pupil-teacher interaction and consequently the personal qualities and skills of teachers are of vital importance. These were explored in question 33 (See Appendix B) which asked schools to list six personal qualities, including acquired skills, which they consider valuable in staff working with disturbed children. The question was open ended and no order of importance in the responses was requested or assumed.

The coding frame adopted, evolved from the responses, is shown below together with the adjusted percentage of schools ($n = 105$) that made nominations in each particular category. (Inverted commas denote actual responses. If two or more nominations from one school were deemed to fall into one category they were treated as one nomination only for that category.)

1 *Maturity of personality*—83%
   This included all responses relating to what many would regard as major and essential components or ingredients of the mature personality, for example stability, independence, self-control, ability to work with others, discretion, humility, experience of life, common sense, and a range of interests.

2 *Warmth to children*—75%
   This included all responses which implied attitudes which would give children the feeling that somebody cares, that is, responses which implied such things as acceptance, affection, caring, concern, 'being on their side', 'willingness to listen', sympathy, love and a parental approach.

3 *Teaching skills*—64%
   This included all responses referring directly to teaching skills or

24

personal abilities which are an integral part of good teaching, for example 'the ability to stimulate others' and 'personal intellectual ability'.

4 *Insight—47%*
This included all responses which suggested an ability on the part of staff possibly to see beyond the surface meanings of behaviour, either intuitively or as a result of study or training, to gain a deeper understanding of the needs and personalities of others, especially the children's, and possibly also of their own.

5 *Sense of humour—48%*
This was almost a self-delineating category, the actual words 'sense of humour' making up almost all of the responses included.

6 *Adaptability or flexibility—42%*
This included all responses suggesting a willingness to adapt or learn, or versatility and imagination.

7 *Commitment—39%*
This included all of those responses which implied a commitment, interest or enthusiasm for the work, a persistence or tenacity in the work, or a personal faith, dedication or philosophy.

8 *Ability to control children—38%*
This included all those responses which referred to such things as consistency, confidence, fairness, management skills, natural authority and strong personality.

9 *Strength and stamina—35%*
This included all responses referring not only to physical strength and stamina but also to reliability or dependability in periods of crisis or stress.

10 *Ability to make relationships—31%*
This included all responses which suggested an ability to be accepted by others as well as to accept others, that is, responses which suggested such things as empathy, sensitivity, ease of contact, understanding, an attractive personality or 'sort of person children choose'.

11 *Moral qualities—15%*
This included all responses referring to the qualities of honesty, integrity, loyalty, conscientiousness and sincerity.

12 *Others—10%*
This included those responses which did not appear to be adequately encompassed by the feel or ambience of other categories, for example, 'lively personality', 'questioning mind', 'a satisfactory sex life'.

Certain of the categories are obviously more difficult to delineate than others, for example 'warmth to children' and 'ability to make relationships' in reference to people working with disturbed children might be considered to be but two faces of the same coin, while others are, and in practice were, far more easily distinguished—for example, a sense of humour. Others might be contributory elements of, or certainly influenced by, others, for example, the strength to keep going may be a function of the strength of commitment or the ability to see the funny side of a possibly stressful situation. It might also be that more distinct qualities might be encompassed by some categories than others—for example, 'maturity' is able to include a far greater number of distinct qualities than a 'sense of humour'. In looking at the outcome here, then one is perhaps better guided to look for an overall feel of the qualities rather than the possible relative importance of particular categories of qualities, although the latter approach may be useful.

In taking an overall view it is worth remembering that the categories were generated from the responses given and that only 2% of the total responses given were not encompassed within eleven main categories. A simple pen picture of the ideal teacher of disturbed pupils, directly encompassing the eleven categories, would be: 'A mature personality incorporating a sense of humour, adaptability, flexibility and basic moral qualities. He will have a warmth towards children coupled with an ability to make two-way relationships with children and adults with some insights into his own and others' needs. He will have the ability to control and teach children, have a personal commitment to the work or some deeper purpose of life and the personal strength and stamina necessary to continue working with disturbed pupils—in short, a pedagogical paragon!

If we cautiously discard the problems and difficulties of apportioning relative importance to these categories, it can be seen that qualities related to *maturity of personality, warmth to children* and *teaching skills* were nominated by more than one half of the responding schools and qualities related to *insight* and *a sense of humour* were nominated by just under one half of the schools. *Moral qualities* were nominated least, receiving less than one half of the nominations of any of the main categories. However, the caution with which the data should be viewed in this way is underlined by the low ranking of *ability to make relationships*, since much of the data relating to treatment (see Chapter 4) suggest that relationships play a major part in most effective treatment programmes.

CHILD CARE STAFF

The qualities of child care staff were explored as they were with teaching staff. Apart from appropriate modification of the category referring to 'teaching skills' the same coding frame evolved for teaching staff was used. The adjusted percentage of schools ($n = 95$) that made nominations in each of the categories is as follows:

1	Warmth to children	81 %
2	Maturity of personality	78 %
3	Insight	45 %
4	Commitment	42 %
5	Child care skills	42 %
6	Sense of humour	41 %
7	Strength and stamina	39 %
8	Adaptability or flexibility	38 %
9	Ability to make relationships	32 %
10	Ability to control children	32 %
11	Moral qualities	22 %
12	Others	8 %

It can be seen that the rankings and response levels for the categories are broadly similar to those for teaching staff and naturally the caveats given in view of the teaching staff must also apply here.

THE SPECIALIST TEAM

The availability of specialist staff is shown in Table 3.1.

Table 3.1   Availability of specialist staff to special schools (Q6) ($n = 114$)

	Available inside school	outside school	in school & outside	Total no. of schools
Psychologist	36	41	10	87
Psychiatrist	46	40	7	93
Psychotherapist	16	9	2	27
School social worker	34	13	10	57

The psychologist   If we assume that those schools that did not respond to this part of the question do not have a psychologist available, then some 76 % of schools have such availability. Less than two-thirds of the not-maintained schools have a psychologist available, compared to 84 % of maintained schools. Of the day schools 89 % responded, compared to 67 % of boarding schools, the predominant pattern of availability for day schools being to have a psychologist available outside the school, while for the boarding schools the availability is equally likely to be outside the school as inside. Of the senior-age schools 70 % responded, compared to 85 % of junior-age schools; junior schools having much greater access to a psychologist outside the school than the senior schools.

The psychiatrist   Again, assuming no response to mean non-availability, 92 % of schools have a psychiatrist available. The position of the maintained/not-maintained schools regarding the availability of a psychiatrist is somewhat reversed with regard to that found for the availability of a psychologist. Here 79 % of maintained schools do have a psychiatrist available compared to 91 % of not-maintained schools. The availability to the not-maintained schools is twice as likely to be outside the school as inside, while this situation is reversed, but to a lesser degree, in the maintained schools.

The psychotherapist   Only 24 % of schools indicated the availability of a psychotherapist. Except for a slightly larger proportion of maintained schools having such availability there were no differences for the different schools.

The school social worker   One half of all schools indicated that they have a school social worker available and for the majority of these the availability is within the school. Maintained schools are more likely than non-maintained schools to have a social worker available (59 % and 41 %) and day schools more likely than boarding schools (64 % and 41 %).

Schools with a school-based social worker ($n = 44$) were asked in question 31 about the social worker's duties. The question sought information on three features that might not necessarily be considered as a normal part of a social worker's duties but which might be appropriate to those of a social worker attached to a school for the maladjusted. In 93 % of the schools, the social worker's duties include 'conducting family case work' and in 73 % they additionally include 'informing the family about the child's educational progress': in 16 % they include, besides these two, 'discussion with groups of families'.

IN-SERVICE TRAINING

Question 35 was an open-ended question and asked schools which had any form of in-service training within the school to indicate its nature. Only 21 % of all schools indicated any formalized system of in-service training within the school, 49 % of schools making no response whatsoever. As it is estimated that nearly 80 % of staff in this work have no appropriate additional training, then these findings might be regarded by some as disappointing. It may be, of course, that schools for the maladjusted do not attach much importance to special training for the work; certainly few schools, in response to question 33, mentioned special training as a feature they considered most valuable in staff, the vast majority specifying characteristics of personality rather than of training. On the other hand, as will be shown later, one third of the schools say that one of the impediments to their work is the difficulty in finding and keeping suitable, trained, or experienced staff.

Only 12 % of schools specified visits to other establishments or attendance to outside courses as forms of in-service training, most of these
having these features additional to a formalized system within the school.
The form of such training most frequently mentioned was discussion with
other members of staff, either informally or at staff or other meetings and
obviously, if this is to be regarded as a valid form of in-service training, then
in-service training must take place in all schools—as one school wrote:
'every minute of the day is in-service training'. While it cannot be denied
that such discussion may result in learning, it could be argued that its lack
of systematic and structured progress negate any suggestion that this might
be seen as a form of training. Clearly, the number of schools who did not
reply to this question—together with those who did not mention
discussion—suggests that in fact the majority of schools do not regard it as
a form of in-service training. Nevertheless, a high proportion of those
responding specified 'discussion' and this clearly indicates that, even if it
cannot be viewed as formal training, it is considered very important in the
furthering of staff knowledge and understanding. Also, as shown later, in
nearly one half of schools, discussion with members of the specialist team is
seen as a valuable form of staff support, and quite possibly embodies a
substantial in-service training element.

Well over one half of the schools (68 %) referred to books, or authors
they had found particularly useful in their work with disturbed pupils
(Q44). Those mentioned covered a wide range and included books or
authors directly associated with disturbed children, psychology, psychiatry, psychotherapy, play therapy, behaviour therapy, remedial education, learning disabilities and testing. Even specific novels were named. No
books or authors were mentioned by 20 % or more of the responding
schools; the four most-mentioned authors were Bettelheim (19 %),
Winnicott (18 %), Dockar-Drysdale (17 %) and Wills (15 %), although it
must be noted that they represent a very small proportion of the total
number of books or authors nominated. Around one quarter of the books
referred to by title (excluding the seven novels specified) are primarily in the
area of education while around 10 % were accounts of work with disturbed
children.

Apart from two sociology texts, the remaining titles were concerned with
psychology, childhood development and childhood problems, and more
direct aspects of treatment, the proportions being around 1:2:1. However,
the overall impression is that, while some schools may refer primarily to
certain authors or books representing a particular approach, for most
schools reading is wide and varied with no particular authors, group of
authors, or viewpoint referred to—a point possibly explained by one
respondent who wrote, 'This is a very heterogeneous group of children with
very complex learning, language and behaviour problems. It is impossible

to list books which would be appropriate to all of their problems, but, in terms of subjects, books on language disorders, learning difficulties at the perceptual and conceptual level, symbolic function, neurological disorders, autism and emotional problems would all contribute to the work.'

SUPPORT FOR STAFF, AND WORK AS A TEAM

Discussions with other members of staff and the specialist team, either formally or informally, formed 95 % of the total responses (87 % of schools) to question 34 concerning ongoing forms of staff support which have been found to be most valuable. Of these schools 65 % mentioned informal discussion with other members of staff and 64 % discussion in staff meetings: both these percentages included 39 % of schools who mentioned both forms of discussion. Discussion with the specialist team was mentioned by 43 % of the schools, although only 6 % did so in isolation from the two forms of discussion previously referred to; 17 % of schools mentioned all three.

One of the areas in which schools were asked to specify any factors which impeded the work of the school was that of support services. Some 62 % responded and, of these, 47 % specified either the lack of, or ineptitude of, the specialist team staff attached to the school. While most specialist teams may be regarded as valuable supporters of staff, a few are seen as an impeding factor. The remaining response referred largely to ineptitude and/or inadequacy of referral agencies and social services.

To enable staff of different disciplines to work as a team the majority of special schools seek to create an atmosphere of friendship and shared responsibility through discussion and the sharing of ideas and decision making. In this respect role clarification within a framework of equality of status is also viewed as important by many schools.

Staff, or features associated with staffing may also impede the work of a school and, indeed, 60 % of schools expressed difficulties in finding and keeping suitable, trained or experienced staff, general staff shortage and frequent changes of staff as impediments to their work.

Special classes and units were asked, 'Who is available within the school and/or outside the school to support and advise the teachers?' Twenty-four per cent of C/Us did not respond or actually stated there was no-one within the school to give such help, but only 10 % responded in this manner with regard to help outside the school. Help within the school was almost entirely confined to colleagues within the C/U or the specialist team, while help outside the school was almost entirely confined to the specialist team, with 82 % of respondents specifying the psychologist with or without other members of the team. Nearly one half of the autonomous units either did not respond or stated that they had no help available within their own unit and, of those who responded they did have such help, 63 % specified the specialist team. The classes and attached units, on the other hand, perceived much greater availability of help within the school, primarily coming from other colleagues rather than the specialist team. There are no differences, however, between the responses of these two types of C/U with regard help available from outside the school.

The ordinary schools were asked with which helping agencies they had effective contact and the results, broken down by the age range of the schools, are shown in Table 3.2 although some of the differences are predictable, the results are of interest since the recipients of Q8 had all been

Table 3.2 Effective contact with helping agencies by junior- and senior-age ordinary schools (in percentages)

	Junior ($n = 76$)	Senior ($n = 53$)
Social services	72·0	85·0
Child guidance unit	63·0	77·0
Probation service**	20·0	62·0
Police**	50·0	85·0
Youth service**	1·0	51·0
Health visitors*	79·0	51·0
School doctor	90·0	77·0
Voluntary societies	21·0	38·0
Other services	10·5	15·0

*$p < 0.001$
**$p < 0.0001$

recommended as doing good work with disturbed pupils. The ordinary schools were also asked which of the following specialists were available to help them in their work with disturbed pupils: school counsellor, educational psychologist, psychiatrist, educational welfare officer and social worker other than the E.W.O. Only 19 % indicated that they had a school counsellor available for such help, and almost all of these were senior-age schools. An educational psychologist was available to all but 3 % of schools and more than two-thirds indicated the availability of each of the remaining specialists. Generally, all the specialists, with the exception of the school's counsellor, were available for such help outside rather than inside of the school, and, with the exception of the educational psychologist, senior-age schools were more likely than junior-age schools to have these specialists available in this way.

SUMMARY

The qualities found most valuable in teachers and child-care staff working with disturbed children broadly coincide with those characteristics generally associated with the mature stable adult, with features of personality being widely recognized as more valuable than specific training or knowledge. The rarity of formalized in-service training programmes possibly reflects this relative lack of stress on specific training or knowledge as the most important requisite for this work. Most schools have a psychologist and psychiatrist available but few have the availability of a pscyhotherapist. One half of the schools have a school social worker available. Members of the specialist team, particularly the psychologist, are seen by many workers in the schools as providing valuable support for the staff.

4 The treatment programme

Over recent years there has been a growing feeling among workers in this field that different types of behavioural or emotional disturbance will require different treatments (for example, Rutter, 1975 and West, 1967), the basic assumption for this has been outlined by one worker as follows:

Within the heterogeneous group categorised 'maladjusted' are pupils who are severely educationally retarded, academically brilliant, neurotic, delinquent, epileptic, psychotic, emotionally deprived, and grossly over-indulged. It would be strange indeed if any one form of treatment could be successfully applied to such a wide range of conditions with an equally wide range of aetiology. (Tait, 1973)

Question 10, which was the major question referring to treatment methods, intended therefore not only to establish which treatment methods are being used in schools for the maladjusted and in what combinations, but also to establish any evidence of differential treatments for particular disorders. Schools were asked to indicate which of twenty-two specified treatment methods they used and to select up to six of those they had found to be most effective for the different types of disorder specified in question 9, plus an extra category of 'all disorders'. (Schools were neither requested to place the treatments they had found to be effective in relation to the different types of disorder in any order of priority nor whether they were currently using them in this way.)

The twenty-two treatment methods were generated by the team from actual references in available literature (see Barker, 1974) and from their own knowledge and experience. The treatments were placed in a random order for the questionnaire.

TREATMENT METHODS USED

Table 4.1 shows the number of schools using each of the treatment methods specified, which are ranked according to analysis A (see p. 35). It can be seen that generally the more specific forms of treatment and those requiring

Table 4.1   Number of schools* using each of the twenty-two treatment methods

Rank	No. of schools	Treatment number	Treatment description
1	112	2	Warm caring attitudes in adult-to-child relationships
2	111	11	Improvement of self-image through success
3	110	7	Remedial teaching in the basic skills
4·5	103	8	Creative work in the arts
4·5	103	13	Opportunity for shared activities with other children
6	101	17	Individual counselling and discussion
7	100	1	A varied and stimulating educational programme
8	97	19	Continuity of child/adult relationships
9	94	18	Freedom to express feelings
10·5	84	22	Firm consistent discipline
10·5	84	20	Teaching of social skills
12	79	21	Group discussion (with teacher or child care staff)
13	78	12	Opportunity for regression
14	57	5	Shared responsibility
15	48	4	Systematic use of incentives and deterrents
16	46	14	Unconditional affection
17	31	9	Individual psychotherapy (under direction of trained therapist)
18·5	28	6	Drug treatment
18·5	28	3	Programmed learning
20	25	10	Techniques of classroom management derived from learning theory
21	16	15	Behaviour therapy with individual pupils (under direction of psychologist)
22	13	16	Group therapy (under direction of trained therapist)

* n = 114

direction by a specialist are used in only one half or less of all the schools. (It must be noted that we are concerned here with the number of schools using a treatment method rather than the number of pupils receiving that treatment. In some instances the actual number of pupils receiving a particular treatment will be very small.)

Shared responsibility and *unconditional affection* which were often, along with psychotherapy, key features stressed by the early pioneers in this work, are also used only in one half or less of all the schools. *Improvement of self image through success, remedial teaching in the basic skills* and *a varied and stimulating educational programme* are all widely used, possibly reflecting the very high proportions of pupils who enter the schools either underachieving and/or requiring remedial help (see Chapter 2) and also the educational bias of teachers and of schools as primarily educational institutions. Along with the more educationally orientated methods, those associated with forming of relationships with others either directly or indirectly—for example, through discussion or shared activities—are also widely used.

The simultaneous use of any treatment with another is of obvious interest and is shown in Table 4.2, the numbers indicating the number of schools using both treatments. The number of schools using each of the treatments (viewed independently, as shown in Table 4.1) is important when referring to this table as the number of schools using both cannot exceed the lower of the two for independent use, for example, *group therapy* is used by only 13 schools and *opportunity for regression* by 78 schools, therefore the maximum number of schools that could use both is 13 (in fact 12 do so). The table can also give a clearer understanding of how schools interpreted each of the treatments, for example as *freedom to express feelings* is used in 71 schools simultaneously with *firm consistent discipline* it can be taken that this freedom takes place within certain constraints rather than with untrammelled permissiveness. (Attempts to identify 'clusters' of treatments according to use are described in Appendix D.)

EFFECTIVENESS OF TREATMENT METHODS

Four basic methods of analysis were used for this part of the question:

Analysis A

This was the primary basic analytic method. The number of nominations for each treatment method as being among the six most effective for a particular disorder were used to produce a ranked order of treatment methods thought to be effective for that disorder. For example *warm caring attitudes in adult to child relationships* was nominated by 75 schools as being among the six most effective treatment methods for conduct disorder pupils and, as this number of nominations exceeded the number of nominations received by any other treatment method for conduct disorders, it was consequently ranked first for effectiveness with conduct disorder pupils.

This method of analysis, however, implicitly embodies a 'most is best' assumption—that that treatment method which is most widely regarded as

Table 4.2 The simultaneous use of treatments

Treatment number	1	2	3	4	5	6	7	8	9	10	11	12	13	14	15	16	17	18	19	20	21
1																					
2	99																				
3	25	28																			
4	40	46	16																		
5	49	56	14	29																	
6	24	28	7	15	18																
7	97	109	28	47	56	28															
8	91	102	23	43	51	26	100														
9	29	31	9	9	16	9	31	30													
10	20	25	10	15	13	8	25	23	5												
11	98	109	28	47	55	28	107	100	29	24											
12	68	78	21	31	45	25	76	74	25	19	76										
13	92	102	27	44	54	26	100	96	28	26	101	70									
14	40	46	11	20	26	14	45	42	12	11	46	40	44								
15	13	16	8	8	11	6	16	15	6	9	16	12	15	5							
16	10	13	7	4	10	5	13	13	9	4	13	12	12	5	6						
17	88	99	25	44	53	27	98	94	30	25	99	69	92	41	15	13					
18	82	93	22	42	50	27	93	89	28	24	91	69	86	43	14	13	86				
19	86	96	25	40	50	27	95	89	29	23	94	68	90	43	14	12	87	83			
20	72	82	22	41	46	27	82	76	23	24	82	61	75	36	13	11	76	74	73		
21	68	76	22	35	48	20	76	73	24	19	78	57	73	32	14	13	76	68	70	60	
22	75	83	24	41	42	24	84	76	23	20	85	54	79	37	12	11	73	71	76	67	63

effective is most effective, and many would contend such a view. Analysis A also ignores that the treatment methods listed may not be available to, or open to use by, all schools; for example, treatment 16 specifies the necessity of direction by a therapist but information from elsewhere in the questionnaire shows that only 27 of the schools have a psychotherapist available to them. Thus the maximum number of schools that could theoretically use treatment 16 is 27, whereas other treatment methods, like *freedom to express feelings*, are theoretically open to use by all schools. Analysis B sought to clarify this issue to some extent.

Analysis B

In this method the number of nominations for each treatment among the six most effective treatments for a disorder was expressed as a percentage of the number of schools that had indicated that they use the treatment. Each treatment was then ranked for each disorder according to this percentage. For example *individual psychotherapy* was nominated by 24 schools as being one of the six most effective treatments for neurotic disorder pupils, which is 77 % of the 31 schools using this treatment. (This is 4 schools more than those reporting that they had a psychotherapist available (see Chapter 3). There may, however, be several valid reasons for this, for example, some teaching staff within the schools might be trained therapists but are not part of the specialist team as specified in question 6, and also a school's psychiatrist may also offer some psychotherapy.) This percentage was higher than any other calculated for neurotic disorders by this method and so it was ranked first for effectiveness with neurotic disorder pupils.

Analysis C

A reverse of the procedure for analysis A was used. Here the disorders were ranked for each treatment rather than the treatments being ranked for each disorder, as in analysis A. For example, *a varied and stimulating educational programme* was nominated by 48 schools as being among the six most effective treatments for educational disorder pupils, more nominations were received for this treatment of the disorder than for any other treatment; therefore educational disorders was ranked first in relation to this treatment.

Analysis D

Analysis D was to analysis C what analysis B was to analysis A. Treatment nominations were expressed as percentages of the number responding for each disorder and the disorders ranked according to the computed percentage. For example, 78 schools nominated treatments for developmental disorder pupils and 46 % (36 schools) of these nominated *opportunity for regression*. For the treatment method *opportunity for regression*

Table 4.3 Nominations and rank order of treatments for disorders

Disorder	Re-plies		1	2	3	4	5	6	7	8	9	10	11	12	13	14	15	16	17	18	19	20	21	22
Conduct	98	No*	33	75	2	22	19	1	23	18	2	11	72	16	31	18	7	3	51	25	37	21	15	64
		A	6	1	20·5	10	12	22	9	13·5	20·5	17	2	15	7	13·5	18	19	4	8	5	10	16	3
		B	11	2	20	5	10	22	16	19	21	6·5	3	17	12	8	6·5	15	4	13	9	14	18	1
		C	2	3	5·5	1	1	6·5	3·5	7	8	1	1	4·5	3	3	1	3	1	3	2	1	2	1
		D	4	4	5·5	1	1	6	5	8	8	3	3	6	3·5	6	3	4	1	4	5	5	4	1
Neurotic	94	No	22	82	1	6	10	7	19	38	24	3	63	30	36	23	3	5	36	38	40	17	19	19
		A	11	1	22	18	16	17	13	4·5	9	20·5	2	8	6·5	10	20·5	19	6·5	4·5	3	15	13	13
		B	15	2	22	20	18	12	12	9	1	21	3	7·5	11	1	17	7·5	10	6	5	16	13	14
		C	6	1	7·5	8	4·5	2	5	1	1	8	3	2	1	1	5	2	2	1	1	5	1	6
		D	7	1	7·5	8	5	3	6	2	1	8	4	2	2	2	6	2	3	2	2	6	2	7
Mixed conduct/ neurotic	91	No	28	78	1	14	12	2	23	26	14	5	69	18	32	19	1	6	32	29	35	20	14	42
		A	8	1	21·5	16	17	20	10	9	14·5	11	2	13	5·5	12	21·5	18	5·5	7	4	11	14·5	3
		B	12	1	22	11	16	20	17	13	5	18	2	15	9	6	21	4	8	10	7	14	19	3
		C	3·5	2	7·5	2	2	5	3	3	2	4	3	3	2	4	7·5	1	4	2	3	3	3	2
		D	5	2	7·5	5	4	5	3·5	6	3	4	2	5	4	4	8	1	4	2	4	4	3	2
Developmental	78	No	28	64	6	11	12	1	28	25	7	4	57	36	23	15	3	2	19	17	28	19	4	25
		A	5	1	17	15	14	22	5	7·5	16	18·5	2	3	9	13	20	21	10·5	12	5	10·5	18·5	7·5
		B	7	1	14·5	12	14·5	22	8	9·5	12	19	2	3	9·5	4	16·5	20	16·5	18	6	12	21	5
		C	3·5	4	3	4	3	7	2	4	5	5	5	1	4	5	5	5	6	4	4	3	8	3
		D	3	3	6	6	3	2	2	5	5	7	5	7	7	5	5	5	7	5	6	3	8	4

Psychosis	57	No	14	37	3	8	5	7	16	8	19	11	24	3	14	15	17	6	15	10	10	25	10	6	18
		A	5	1	20·5	14·5	19	16	6	14·5	9·5	4	3	20·5	9·5	11·5	6	17·5	7	12·5	12·5	5	12·5	17·5	5
		B	14	3·5	17·5	11·5	19	6	17·5	22	9·5	11	8	6	9·5	3·5	7	2	2	15·5	17·5	2	15·5	20·5	8
		C	7	8	4	7	7	3	2	7	6	2	8	5·5	6	4	8	6	1·5	6	7	5	7	5	7
		D	6	7	4	7	6	2	2	8	4	3	8	5·5	4	1	6	1·5	3	3	7	1	7	5	5

Personality	57	No	13	43	2	11	10	3	19·5	6	20	8	33	3	16	18	13	6	17	20	14	12	19
		A	11·5	1·5	21·5	14	15	19·5	5	17·5	4·5	16	2	19·5	9	7	11·5	17·5	8	4·5	10	13	6
		B	18	1·5	21	6	14	22	17·5	12	5	14	19	14	4	1·5	12	9	9	15	13	16·5	9
		C	8	5	5	4	3	8	8	8	3	5	6	3	5	6	5	3	5	8	6	4	5
		D	8	5	5·5	3	2	4	3	8	3	4	6	3·5	3	3·5	3	1·5	3	7	2	1	3·5

Neurological	60	No	25	41	9	12	4	17	15	14	4	4	8	29	9	18	10	3	1	12	12	18	21	4	20
		A	3	1	15·5	12·5	19	8	9	10·5	19	10·5	17	2	15·5	6·5	14	21	22	15	15	6·5	4	19	5
		B	6·5	2	3·5	6·5	21·5	1	15	15	17·5	15	3·5	5	19	13	10	12	20	17·5	17·5	10	10	22	8
		C	5	7	2	3	8	1	6	8	6	8	6	7	7	6	7	4	7	6	6	4	7	4	4
		D	2	6	2	2	8	1	4	7	6	3	2	7	7	5	7	4	7	8	6	8	8	1	3·5

Educational	69	No	48	42	15	11	6	0	58	29	2	18	2	10	59	1	18	4	1	22	5	27	7	4	17
		A	3	4	10	11	14	22	2	5	18	12	5	1	20	16·5	20	1	20	6	13	16·5	9
		B	4	6	1	9	13	22	2·5	7·5	17·5	5	21	17·5	14	17·5	15·5	7·5	15·5	8	19·5	11
		C	1	8	1	6	6	8	1	2	2	7	2	8	7	8	8	8	8	5	8	8	8
		D	1	8	1	7	7	8	1	1	7	7	1	8	8	8	8	5	8	3	8	6	6

All disorders	81	No	41	72	3	11	15	2	21	19	10	6	65	15	25	3	17	5	17	32	9	9	43
		A	4	1	20·5	14	12·5	22	8	9	15	18·5	2	12·5	7	20·5	10·5	6	10·5	5	16·5	16·5	3
		B	5	1	20	13	10	22	15	17·5	15	11·5	2	15	11·5	15	17·5	18·5	17·5	7	20	20	3
		C	2	4	4	2	2	5·5	5	6·5	5	4	3	6	6	5·5	4	5·5	4	8	8	5	2
		D	2	1	5	1	6·5	5·5	3	1	4	4	1	7	7	1	2	1	5	3	8	8	2

* No = Number of schools nominating. A, B, C, D = Ranks of treatment and disorder according to the appropriate method of analysis (A, B, C or D). Rankings for C and D are without the inclusion of the all disorders category except for those referring to that category.

no other disorder group exceeded a similarly calculated percentage and consequently the developmental disorder group was ranked first for this treatment.

Of the four methods analyses A and B would appear to be the most useful in aiding the construction of a treatment programme in that they embody an ordering of judged effectiveness of treatments in relation to each other for particular disorders. Analyses C and D, on the other hand, give no indication of the relative judged effectiveness of a treatment, only that if a particular treatment is used (although, in some cases, not widely thought to be effective), which disorders it is likely to be most effective with. Analyses A and B compare treatment against treatment for each disorder category, analyses C and D compare disorder against disorder for each treatment.

The number of schools nominating each treatment as being effective with each of the specified disorder categories, the number of schools that made nominations for each of the specified disorder categories, and the rank order positions of treatments for each of the four methods of analysis are shown in Table 4.3. Comment on such complex data must inevitably be limited in this report and will be restricted to the group's conduct, neurotic, mixed conduct/neurotic, all disorders and some overall impressions. There is sufficient information in Tables 4.1 and 4.3 for the reader to follow almost any specific line of interest in the data accrued from question 10. Some notes of caution on possible interpretations of the rank order positions is necessary, however, particularly those related to analyses C and D. Firstly, a high ranking may be obtained from a very low number of nominations or derived percentage; for example the mixed conduct neurotic group are ranked first under analysis D for the effectiveness of treatment 16 (group therapy) although the percentage involved is only 6·6. Secondly, the rank order positions ignore the range of nominations or derived percentages involved; treatment 7 (remedial teaching), for example, by analysis D has a range of some 73 %, while treatment 16 (group therapy) by the same analysis has a range of only 5 %. Thirdly, the rank order positions ignore the within range differences—for example, under analysis D for the treatment *remedial teaching in the basic skills*, there is a difference of 48 % between the first two ranked disorders (educational disorders clearly being ranked first), while for *creative work in the arts* there is a difference of only 2 % between the first two ranked.

Table 4.4 shows a matrix of the correlation coefficients of the rankings of treatments for the various disorder categories. The left-hand lower half of the matrix shows the coefficients for rankings derived from analysis A and the right-hand upper half of the matrix those derived from analysis B. The higher a positive coefficient in this matrix, the greater the likelihood that the treatments considered to be effective for the two disorders will coincide.

Table 4.4 Correlation coefficients of treatment rankings

	Conduct	Neurotic	Mixed C/N	Development	Psychosis	Personality	Neurological	Educational	All disorders
Conduct		0·09		0·38	0·26	0·58	0·41	0·37	0·66
Neurotic	0·66		0·73	0·39	0·51	0·56	−0·15	−0·24	0·49
Mixed C/N	0·86	0·83		0·54	0·36	0·57	0·03	0·13	0·82
Developmental	0·79	0·74	0·83		0·43	0·47	0·23	0·41	0·56
Psychosis	0·74	0·85	0·88	0·81		0·73	0·43	−0·13	0·32
Personality	0·81	0·87	0·90	0·77	0·90		0·01	−0·15	0·51
Neurological	0·75	0·56	0·76	0·73	0·80	0·65		0·48	0·14
Educational	0·77	0·48	0·70	0·72	0·58	0·55	0·73		0·36
All disorders	0·92	0·79	0·94	0·86	0·86	0·84	0·73	0·76	
Used	0·82	0·79	0·87	0·85	0·75	0·81	0·74	0·81	0·85

Analysis A

Analysis B

Low or negative coefficients show there is little or no coincidence between the treatments considered effective for the two disorders in question.

TREATMENTS FOR CONDUCT DISORDERS

Firm consistent discipline, improvement of self-image through success, individual counselling and discussion, warm caring attitudes in adult-to-child relationships, and the *systematic use of incentives or deterrents* achieve generally high rankings by any of the four methods of analysis.* On the other hand, low rankings are achieved by *individual psychotherapy, drug treatment, programmed learning, opportunities for regression, creative work in the arts* and *group therapy.*†

There are some particularly notable changes in the rankings of some treatments under analyses A and B. *Systematic use of incentives and deterrents, techniques of classroom management derived from learning theory* and *behaviour therapy* are all in the six ranked highest by analysis B, although by analysis A they are ranked tenth, seventeenth and eighteenth respectively. This suggests that, although these treatments are not widely used, they are considered by those who do use them to be effective with conduct disordered pupils.

Table 4.4 shows that there is little relationship between rankings of the perceived effectiveness of treatments by analysis B for conduct disorder and those for neurotic disorders (by analysis A the correlation coefficient between these two is also lower than any other involving conduct disorders) and that the greatest relationship, by either analysis, for the treatment rankings for conduct disorder is with those for the *all disorders* category. This latter finding may be a reflection of the predominance of conduct disorders within the schools and possibly their influence on the total treatment programmes offered.

TREATMENTS FOR NEUROTIC DISORDERS

Using the same cut-off points for the mean rankings as used for conduct disorders, the highest rankings are attained by *warm caring attitudes in adult-to-child relationships, individual counselling and discussion, individual psychotherapy, improvement of self-image through success, continuity of child/adult relationships, freedom to express feelings, opportunity for shared activities with other children, creative work in the arts* and *opportunity for regression.* Low ranked treatments are *programmed learning, techniques of classroom management derived from learning theory, systematic use of*

---

*   The mean of the four rankings for each of these treatments is 5 or below. As the rankings for analyses A and B have a range of 1 to 22 and those for C and D have a range of only 1 to 8, this simple mean gives extra weight to analyses A and B which are thought to provide better guidance to overall effectiveness (see page 40).

†   The mean of the four rankings for each of these treatments is 10 or above (NB the highest mean possible is 15)

incentives or deterrents, behaviour therapy, shared responsibility, remedial teaching in the basic skills, teaching of social skills, and *firm consistent discipline.*

The ranking of treatments by analysis B for neurotic disorders is negatively correlated with those for neurological and educational disorders, and coefficients for these groups under analysis A are also lower than those for any other groups. As stated in the previous section, the correlation of treatment ranking by analysis B for the neurotic and conduct disorder group is almost zero and under analysis B the coefficient is lower than all but neurological and educational disorders.

TREATMENTS FOR MIXED CONDUCT/NEUROTIC DISORDERS

Treatments generally highly ranked for the mixed conduct neurotic disorders are *warm caring attitudes in adult-to-child relationships, improvement of self-image through success, firm consistent discipline, opportunity for shared activities with other children, continuity of child/adult relationships,* and *freedom to express feelings,* and *individual counselling and discussion.* Lowly ranked are *programmed learning, behaviour therapy, drug treatment,* and *techniques of classroom management derived from learning theory.* There is an almost zero correlation between the ranking of treatments by analysis B for this group and the neurological group and a quite low correlation with those for educational disorders.

There are two particularly large changes in the rankings according to analyses A and B. Under analysis A, group therapy attains only eighteenth rank but under analysis B is ranked fourth. Similarly, individual psychotherapy moves up from a ranking of 14·5 under analysis A to a ranking of 5 under analysis B. Unconditional affection makes a less dramatic change from a ranking of 12 under analysis A to 6·5 under analysis B.

ALL DISORDERS

Overall, the highest ranked treatments for all disorders are *warm caring attitudes in adult-to-child relationships, improvement of self-image through success, firm consistent discipline, a varied and stimulating educational programme,* and *continuity of child/adult relationships.* The overall lowest ranked are *drug treatment, teaching of social skills, programmed learning, group discussion, behaviour therapy, systematic use of incentives and deterrents* and *opportunity for regression.*

Table 4.4 shows that both under analysis A and analysis B, the greatest correlation between the ranking of treatments for this *all disorder* category and the other disorders is that for mixed conduct/neurotic group followed, again under both analyses, by the conduct disorder group. There is, using analysis B almost zero correlation between the *all disorder* treatment ranking and those for the neurological disorder group.

One particularly noticeable change in rankings between analyses A and B occurs for *group therapy* which attains a rank of 4 under analysis B while only attaining a rank of 18·5 under analysis A. Several other treatments (7, 8, 9, 10 and 18) have a difference of seven or more rank places for the two analyses A and B.

OVERALL IMPRESSIONS AND COMMENTS

Two treatments clearly stand out from the others in their overall perceived effectiveness: *warm caring attitudes in adult-to-child relationships* and *improvement of self-image through success*. Under analyses A and B they are in the first six ranked for every disorder specified with one exception. *Improvement of self-image* was ranked seventh under analysis B for psychosis. Importantly, under analyses C and D they are regarded as being particularly effective in the treatment of the three largest groups of disorders within the schools, the conduct, the neurotic and the mixed conduct/neurotic disorders. They were also, it may be remembered from Table 4.1, the two most widely used treatments in school and, as they consistently retain a high ranking in analysis B (which implicitly weights against the most widely used treatments) this is almost certainly a reflection of their perceived effectiveness. The only other treatment which attains generally high rankings of effectiveness across all of the disorders specified is *continuity of child/adult relationships* which clearly underlines the importance of relationships in any effective treatment programme for maladjusted children.

At the other end of the scale none of the specified treatments attains consistently low rankings across all of the disorders. Two here, however, also tend to stand out from the others in that they have generally very low rankings apart from those referring to one or two of the minority disorders. The first of these is *drug treatment* which is considered to be particularly effective only for neurological disorders. The second is *programmed learning* which is considered to be generally effective only with the educational disorder group, although via analysis B it attains high rankings for the personality and neurological disorder groups. This finding is quite interesting. Educational disorders were defined in the questionnaire as being 'not secondary to subnormality or maladjustment', and, although 92 % of pupils were seen as underachieving according to their potential on entry to the schools, only 4 % were put in this category. This evidence strongly suggests therefore that the learning difficulties of maladjusted pupils are quite different from those of pupils who are either not maladjusted or whose maladjustment is secondary to their learning difficulties.

Using analysis A the treatments schools see as being most effective with any of the disorders broadly coincide with those most widely used in the schools. To the extent that schools actively choose the treatments they use, this is to be expected. One could reasonably expect their choice of treatments to be based upon some estimate of their effectiveness, albeit in reference to problems of practical application—for example, staffing—for, as shown earlier, the treatments most widely used are, in almost every case, those that can be operated without specialist help or knowledge and could be adopted by most practising teachers.

The influence on treatment programmes of the three numerically largest groups in the schools, the conduct, neurotic and mixed conduct/neurotic, which account for 76% of the total population, is reflected in the correlations between these groups and treatments *used* and the *all disorder* categories shown in Table 4.4. The highest coefficients with *used* and *all disorders* under both analysis A and analysis B are those referring to the mixed conduct/neurotic disorders. In the same way conduct disorders attains relatively high coefficients, second highest under both analyses with *all disorders* and third with *used*. Neurotic disorders in this respect attain lower correlations and so the results suggest that the total programme in schools tends to be mainly in reference to the problems associated with conduct disorders but the prevalence of neurotic problems dictate that these cannot be ignored. The relatively low correlations between the treatment rankings for the conduct and neurotic disorder groups and the higher correlations between the conduct and the mixed conduct/neurotic disorders give strong support for this suggestion.

In the data there is evidence of differential treatment according to type of disorder. Treatments associated with the behaviourist and learning theory approaches tend to have much higher rankings in reference to conduct disorders than they do in reference to neurotic or mixed conduct/neurotic disorders. On the other hand, treatments associated with the more psychodynamic approaches tend to have high rankings in reference to the neurotic and mixed conduct/neurotic disorders—particularly the neurotic—than they do in reference to conduct disorders. The treatment rankings for educational disorders have relatively low correlations with those for other disorders and notably with those disorders which many feel have a greater emotional or psychological basis than others—the neurotic, psychotic and personality disorders—and higher correlations with conduct, developmental and neurological disorders. The treatments for the neurologically disordered also have low correlations with those for the neurotic and personality disorders but, interestingly, have high correlations with those for the psychotic in addition to conduct and educational disorders. All of the correlations of treatment rankings for the various disorders under analysis A are statistically highly significant and this would seem to indicate that in most schools different treatments for the different disorders is one of emphasis rather than of type. Under analysis B, however, which takes usage into account (This method shows that schools adopting a particular approach do not necessarily see it as being equally effective with all of the disorders.), the position clearly seems to be that the psychodynamic treatments are viewed as effective for the treatment of neurotic type symptoms with or without the presence of conduct disorder symptoms, while behaviourist approaches are regarded as effective for treating conduct disorder symptoms that are not accompanied by symptoms of a neurotic disorder.

INCENTIVES AND DETERRENTS

The special schools were also asked what incentives and deterrents, if any, they had found to be most effective with the various types of disorder. The question (Q 15) was open ended and space was provided for the nomination of three incentives and three deterrents for each disorder. Sixteen per cent of the schools made no response whatsoever, 21 % did not answer the question as posed but made a general comment about the problem of incentives and deterrents in relation to disturbed children, and a further 8 % gave nominations only for. all disturbed children. Thus nearly one half (45 %) of all the responding schools were reluctant to specify incentives and deterrents for the various types of disorder, most of these being reluctant to respond or even perhaps to think in terms of incentives and deterrents at all in relation to disturbed children.

Most of those making a general comment referred to the importance of interpersonal relationships and the subsequent efficacy of approval and disapproval as management techniques but were not inclined to call these incentives and deterrents, for example; 'We try not to define incentives and deterrents too closely and I think it would be true to say that we never punish in an obvious sense. The incentive which is most valuable is individual and group approval. Temporary withdrawal of privileges is a sign of disapproval, but I hesitate to call this a deterrent.'; 'Because of the importance given to fostering relationships, the most important form of deterrent is that a child has let someone down by his unacceptable behaviour.'; 'I do not believe that either incentives or deterrents have ever had any important part to play in the management of pupils at X school . . . It could, I suppose, be said that affection and caring given to disturbed boys are incentives, but they are always unconditional and unrelated to behaviour at X school.'

As can be seen in Table 4.5, however, most of the schools who did respond to the question did view aspects or consequences of sound child/adult relationships in terms of incentives and deterrents. Table 4.5 shows the major categories into which most of the responses to question 15 could be gathered for the conduct disorder, neurotic disorder and all disturbed groups. The percentages in the table are the number of

Táble 4.5 Incentives and deterrents found to be effective with conduct disordered, neurotic disordered, and all disturbed children (Q15)

	Conduct disorders (n = 59) %	Neurotic disorders (n = 48) %	All disturbed (n = 54) %
Incentives			
Child/adult relationships	27	56	39
Approval and praise	53	42	52
Increased status and specific privileges and rewards	89	44	54
Fostering success and self-esteem	19	12	22
Counselling, discussion and encouragement of self-knowledge	0	40	7
Deterrents			
Disapproval/displeasure	47	29	35
Loss of status and specific privileges and rewards	68	12	39
Specific sanctions	39	10	28
Physical control/restraint, isolation, etc.	25	8	11
Counselling and discussion	8	0	0

nominations falling into that category expressed as a percentage of the number of schools responding on the disorder in question. For various reasons (for example, schools could give up to three incentives and deterrents) these percentages should be regarded as indices of emphasis and not as accurate quantitative data. Here, as in question 10, we find evidence of differential treatment according to type of disorder. Firstly, there is a relative lack of emphasis on deterrents for neurotic disorders, one third of the respondents for this group did not specify any deterrents, three of these commenting: '. . . any deterrent builds defences which makes progress difficult . . .'; '. . . only positive advances made. No deterrents.', and '. . . non-effective—these children require incentives'. (Of those responding to the 'all disorders' category, 24% did not specify deterrents.)

Recognizable increases or decreases in status and the awarding or removing of specific privileges were generally viewed as effective with the conduct disorder group but less so with the neurotic group. Features of child/adult relationships were specified more often as effective with neurotic disorders than conduct disorders. Finally, and very interestingly, while many schools mentioned counselling, discussion and the encouragement of self knowledge as an effective incentive for children with neurotic disorders, none did so for children with conduct disorders, indeed a small group mentioned these as an effective deterrent for children with conduct disorders. It may be remembered that in data accruing from question 10 individual counselling and discussion was widely thought to be particularly effective for both of these groups, and perhaps more so for the conduct disorder group than the neurotic disorder group. The data suggest that this effectiveness comes through its power as a deterrent for conduct disorders and as an incentive for neurotic disorders.

MEDICAL AND PSYCHOLOGICAL TREATMENT

The data from question 10 show that, although the majority of special schools have access to a psychologist or psychiatrist (see Chapter 3), they do not play a major part in the overall treatment programme. Moreover, the percentage of maladjusted pupils receiving specific medical and psychological treatments is small (see Table 4.6). Few schools have a majority of their pupils receiving any one of these treatments (individual psychotherapy—62 schools; group psychotherapy—93 schools; behaviour therapy—89 schools; drug treatment—57 schools). It follows then that, while 46 schools have some of their pupils receiving individual psychotherapy and 51 schools have some of their pupils receiving drug treatment, only 15 and 19 respectively have some of their pupils receiving group psychotherapy and/or behaviour therapy. It is the high proportion of schools having none of their pupils receiving each of the treatments that largely accounts for the substantial differences between the means and medians shown in Table 4.6

TREATMENT IN THE SCHOOL AS A COMMUNITY

In schools for the maladjusted, the treatment programme may operate on

Table 4.6   Percentage of pupils receiving medical and psychological treatment (Q17)

Treatment	Mean %	Median %
Individual psychotherapy	12·0	0·4
Group psychotherapy	4·0	0·1
Behaviour therapy	8·0	0·1
Drug treatment	4·0	0·4

(Number of schools = 108)

at least three levels. Firstly, there is the individual level whereby the unique qualities of each pupil are emphasized and consequently a unique treatment programme is demanded for each child. While this approach was recognized as essential to some degree in any treatment programme, it was not investigated in the questionnaire. This was basically because an investigation at this level would be least productive in meeting the project aim of offering guidance to teachers; in short, to say that it is all individual offers little guidance, true though it may be! Secondly, there is the 'type of problem' level, which is more or less the level investigated by question 10; that is, quite simply, different problems require different treatments. Thirdly, there is the 'school as a unit' level, whereby the ongoing organization and structure of the school is directed towards the overall needs of its pupils. This third level is discussed in this section. However, it is recognized that, although the three levels may be viewed separately, in practice there is much overlap.

We have already seen much data with implications for this section, for example: the schools are small and well staffed by the standards of normal schools; the majority have residential provisions, most have access to specialist help of various kinds, and much in Chapter 5 on the educational programme will also be relevant. But here we are concerned with questions that refer more directly to the school as a community.

Question 11 asked schools to weight certain widely recognized approaches or techniques according to their importance in running a community for disturbed pupils. A five-point scale was used (5 = most important; 1 = least important) and the features and results are shown in Table 4.7.

Table 4.7   Importance of specified features in running a community (Q11)

	Median	Mean
Accepting relationships	4·8	4·6
Gaining of insight (pupil)	4·1	4·1
Routine and discipline	3·6	3·5
Scholastic progress	3·6	3·5
Expressive work in the arts	3·0	2·8
Opportunities for regression	2·7	2·6
Pupil involvement in management	2·2	2·1

There is at least an intuitive congruence between this ranking and that found for the approaches found most effective under analysis A for *all disorders* in question 10, which were, in order of rank: warm caring attitudes in adult to child relationships; improvement of self-image through success; firm consistent discipline; a varied and stimulating educational programme; continuity of child-adult relationships; and individual counselling and discussion. In both we find evidence of great and widespread emphasis on relationships but within a structure of routine and discipline and educational concern. While there was no highly analogous approach in question 10 to *gaining of insight (pupil)*, the high ranking of this approach perhaps gives some indication of the possible purpose or aim of *individual counselling and discussion* and, more tenuously, *improvement of self-image through success* which were both highly ranked in analysis A for all disorders. The low rankings here: *expressive work in the arts, opportunities for regression*, and *pupil involvement in management* are reflected by the low rankings of their counterparts for *all disorders* in question 10: *creative work in the arts, opportunity for regression* and *shared responsibility*. Here again we find evidence that the importance of certain approaches advocated by the early pioneers of the work (see Bridgeland, 1971) are currently viewed as less important.

There were no notable differences among schools for different age ranges or of different maintaining authority but there were slight tendencies for day schools to weight *routine and discipline* and *expressive work in the arts* more highly and to give lower weightings to *opportunities for regression* than boarding schools.

How schools allocate their time is obviously important, but clearly the amount of time available for working with pupils will differ considerably between day and boarding schools. Boarding schools generally have twice as much time available to them for working with pupils as do day schools (see Table 4.8). (The data for mixed day-boarding schools and for boarding only schools were very similar, suggesting that the former referred to their boarding pupils when answering this question.) Day schools, perhaps naturally, allocate proportionately more of their available time to school work in the classroom and less to free leisure activities than boarding schools.

The schools were also asked to indicate to what degree pupils were free to choose whether to participate in these activities. They were given a choice of three responses: free choice, limited choice and no choice. Most schools for each activity gave only one of these responses but some did give more than one, and the percentages in Table 4.8 refer to the percentage of schools that gave single responses, that is, schools that made more than one response are omitted. The table shows that only in leisure activity time was free choice on the part of pupils widespread, for all other activities the usual practice was for pupils to have limited choice or none.

It has been seen that *shared responsibility* is used in only one half of schools, that *pupil involvement in management* is not widely regarded as an

Table 4.8 Allocation of school time and degree of pupil choice (Q12)

	Schools boarding (n = 64)		day (n = 26)		Choice free	limited	none
	hrs	min.	hrs	min.	%	%	%
School work in the classroom	4	27	3	0	1	44	43
Organized leisure activities	1	36	1	0	44	45	5
Free leisure activities	3	11		58	88	6	3
Meals and snacks	1	57		39	5	40	53
Personal physical care		55		6	7	41	46
Communal living duties		48		55	4	38	51

important feature in running a community for disturbed children, and now we see that in most school activities pupils have either only limited choice or none. Then how do pupils participate? Question 16 asked this question, firstly, in the running of the community and, secondly in their own treatment programme. To the first part of this question 28 % of schools either did not respond or actually stated that pupils played no part in the running of the community. Most of the remainder said that pupils organized games, clubs and other such activities. Some schools referred to participation through a formal school council and a few of these mentioned actual decision-making powers; one school indeed stated that the council even decided 'priorities in spending'. For pupil participation in their own treatment programme, 39 % of schools either did not respond or stated that pupils did not participate in this way. Most other responses referred to participation via discussion, either formally or informally and at· an individual or group level. The remainder included such things as pupil self-help, either directly—for example, through agreements and contracts, or indirectly—for example, by being informed or made aware of the treatment programme. However, the overall tenor of the responses to these two sections was that where pupil participation occurs it is, except in a small minority of cases, on a very limited level.

Many of the routines and procedures of normal school life, particularly in the boarding schools, may be open to therapeutic use. The schools were asked in what practical ways they used some of these to further the emotional well-being of pupils. Those specified were: personal possessions, care of surroundings, routine physical care, minor illness and ailments, going to bed, clothing, meal times and getting up. The responses show that most schools see and use opportunities in these procedures to further the emotional well-being of their pupils.

Overall there is an emphasis on the need to develop or create a respect and care for one's own and others' possessions and for the surroundings in which one lives. Opportunities for the development of personal pride, personal value and independence occur in providing routine and physical care, the provision of personal clothing, and the treatment of minor illnesses and ailments. Opportunities for staff to show care and to give extra attention are seen to exist particularly in the treatment of minor illnesses and ailments, at meal times, and, in the boarding schools, going to bed and getting up. For both going to bed and getting up a small group of schools stressed the need for flexibility, while a comparably small group stressed the need for a regular routine.

WORK WITH FAMILIES

Over one half the schools, in response to question 43, specified factors in the family that impede the work of the school. The majority of these responded either that families were the cause or maintaining feature of many children's difficulties or that families were hostile to, or uninterested in, what the school was trying to do. The remainder specified that they neither have sufficient time nor facilities to carry out useful work with families. Thus high proportion of schools felt that family influences could actually impede their work. Nearly all schools (95 %) made contact with the family prior to the child's admission to the school and over three-quarters (79 %) made use of visits to organized school events to establish and maintain contact with families.

Day schools were more likely than boarding schools to use formal visits to discuss progress (93 % and 74 %), but boarding schools tended to make more use of social visits (88 % and 75 %). Home visits by a social worker were used slightly more by day schools than by boarding schools (89 % and 70 %) and more by maintained than those not maintained (83 % and 63 %). Group parent meetings were not widely used (only 19 % of schools) and were more likely to be used in day schools rather than boarding schools (36 % and 9 %) and in primary schools rather than senior schools (43 % and 4 %). Boarding schools were very much more likely to use written reports than day schools (75 % and 48 %). In addition to these 44 % of the schools used other methods of establishing and maintaining contact with families, the most frequent of these being by telephone.

In viewing this information from question 30 it needs to be remembered firstly, that the question was concerned with use and not frequency, and secondly that senior age schools are predominantly boarding schools. The overall impression from the data is that face-to-face contact with the family, either at the school or via a social worker, in the home, is used more by day schools than boarding schools, which perhaps try to counter this by using written reports more than do day schools. For many reasons, for example geographical location, it is perhaps to be expected that group parent meetings are rare in the boarding school, but the comparative rarity in senior schools does not appear to be just a function of the senior school/boarding school ratio.

ASSESSMENT AND RECORDING OF PERSONAL/SOCIAL PROGRESS

Ninety per cent of the schools responded to question 37 which was concerned with how often pupils' personal/social progress is assessed and recorded. Of the respondents, 22 % indicated that this progress is assessed and recorded *as occasion arises* with no regularized assessment or recording. Another 40 % indicated *as occasion arises* but that this was in addition to a regular schedule of assessment. Twenty-eight per cent of schools responding to the question assess and record monthly or less, 32 % of these in conjunction with *as occasion arises*. Thirty-four per cent assess and record once per term, 63 % of these in conjunction with *as occasion arises*, and 17 % do this work annually with 59 % of these also doing it *as occasion arises*. Compared to the assessment and recording of educational progress (see Chapter 5) the general impression is that the assessment and recording of personal/social progress is more frequent but less regularized than it is for educational progress.

Contributors to this assessment in more than one half of the schools include child care staff and members of the specialist team along with the teaching staff. In another 30 % the assessment is done by the teaching and child care staffs, without the involvement of the specialist team. Less than 5 % of schools use the teaching staff only for assessment of pupil personal/social progress compared to 47 % who use only teachers for assessing educational progress. Thus assessment and recording of personal/social progress is, in almost all schools, very much a team responsibility, a feature that was emphasized in methods of enabling staff of different disciplines to work as a team (see Chapter 3). Only 29 % of schools use standardized measures of social and/or personal readjustment.

The frequency of assessment in classes/units (C/Us) was not investigated, but C/Us were asked which people and tests were used in the assessment of their pupils for selection for admission to the C/U, during a pupil's attendance, and for re-entry to the ordinary school system. The people most used at these stages are teachers-in-charge of the provisions, heads of schools and psychologists. The psychologist is used by nearly 80 % of all C/Us for the selection of pupils, by 66 % for assessment during stay, and by 46 % for the re-entry of pupils to ordinary school and is more widely used at all three stages by the units than by the classes. Pastoral care staff, school counsellors, and social workers are not used at any of the stages by one third or more of the C/Us The use of standard IQ tests and attainment tests is reported in Chapter 5.

SUMMARY

Taking schools for the maladjusted as a group, the overall treatment programme is based upon a foundation of warm and caring attitudes in adult-to-child relationship and efforts to improve the self-image of pupils through success. The continuity of adult/child relationships is viewed as being effective in the treatment of all types of disorder and individual counselling and discussion is seen as being particularly effective with the three main groups of pupils, the conduct, neurotic and mixed conduct/neurotic disorders. The schools, considered as a group, lean towards a structured, disciplined and adult-directed approach rather than to one of freedom or permissiveness. Pupil direction, shared responsibility, pupil involvement in management, and—in all but leisure activities—the degree to which pupils can choose to participate are limited. The management of pupils is seen to be facilitated by most schools in the quality of the child/adult relationship developed and maintained. This overall programme of the schools in general resembles more closely the approaches thought to be effective with the conduct disorder group than those thought to be effective with the neurotic disorder group.

5 The educational programme

THE FORMAL CURRICULUM

Table 5.1 shows the subjects taught ranked according to the number of schools teaching the subject. As can be seen, the most widely taught subjects are *English language, Mathematics, Arts and crafts* and *Physical education and allied subjects*, each generally being taught as subjects in their own right. *Geography, History* and *English literature* are also widely taught but are more likely to be taught as part of an integrated studies programme. The data suggest that in a typical school these core subjects are likely to be supported by up to four other common school subjects. The least widely taught subjects tend to be those not taught widely in ordinary schools either, or subjects that essentially demand a specialist trained teacher. In view of their widely recognized therapeutic qualities it is perhaps worth noting that *Music* is ranked only thirteenth and *Drama* and movement only fourteenth of the twenty subjects specified although they are taught in over 70% of all schools and in all but three of the junior schools (85% of all junior schools). (Sixty-one per cent of the fifty-one senior schools teach Music and 59% teach Drama.)

Technical drawing, Careers, Preparation for parenthood and *Commercial subjects* are not taught in any primary school but, with the exception of *Commercial subjects*, are fairly common in the senior and all-age range schools. *Health education* is taught in over 80% of senior and all-age range schools but in only 35% of primary schools. Apart from these perhaps expected differences, there are no other differences worthy of note between the primary and senior-age schools.

The ranking of subjects taught in the special classes and units closely resembles that for the special schools, the only notable exception being that *Domestic subjects* is more highly ranked (8th), although less widely taught (56%). This is basically because the classes and units tend to teach fewer subjects than the special schools with only *English language, Mathematics* and *Arts and crafts* being widely taught.

Table 5.1   Subjects taught in special schools (Q20)

Rank	Subject	Number of schools teaching subject			
		Taught in own right	Part of integrated study	Both	TOTAL (*n* = 111)*
1	English language	65	33	13	111
1	Mathematics	76	21	14	111
3	Arts & crafts	67	21	21	109
3	P.E. and allied subjects	81	17	11	109
5	Geography	42	51	10	103
6	History	40	54	8	102
7	English literature	45	47	7	99
8	Science	43	46	4	93
9	Environmental studies	29	58	4	91
10	Woodwork/metalwork	64	21	2	87
11	Religious or moral education	36	44	4	84
12	Health education (incl. sex education)	29	50	3	82
13	Music	51	23	5	79
14	Drama and movement	48	27	3	78
15	Careers	41	33	1	75
16	Domestic subjects	49	17	7	73
17	Preparation for parenthood	10	33	4	47
18	Technical drawing	33	11	1	45
19	Commercial subjects	15	10	0	25
20	Modern language	18	3	6	21

*   3 schools did not complete this question.

ALLOCATION OF CLASSROOM TIME

As was shown in Chapter 4 (see Table 4.8), the amount of time allocated for school work in the classroom differs between day and boarding schools. The average time allocated for day schools is 3 hours while for boarding schools it is slightly under 4½ hours. It is interesting to note that boarding schools that take some day pupils allocate, like the boarding only schools, slightly under 4½ hours for classroom work, and an investigation to see if this has adverse or any other consequences for the day pupils would be of some interest. Although the amount of time available for schoolwork differs between the day and boarding schools the proportions of that time spent in different subject areas is very similar. Table 5.2 shows the overall

Table 5.2   Percentage of school time allocated to subject areas (Q22)

Percentage of available time	Subject area
39	Fundamental skills
15	Creative arts (painting, writing, music, drama, etc.)
13	Humanities (literature, history, moral education, etc.)
12	P.E. and allied activities
8	Handicrafts (wood, metal)
7	The sciences
6	Others

proportions of time allocated to different subject areas and these are broadly the same for all schools.

TEACHING METHODS

Question 19, which was concerned with teaching methods, was divided into two parts: one related to pupils under 11 years of age, and the other to those above the age of 11.

Less than 5 % of the schools ($n = 87$) indicated that their teaching was largely specialized for the under-11 age group, although 58 % indicated that they used some specialization. For the overall age group 12 % of the schools ($n = 96$) responded that their teaching was largely specialized and 78 % responded that they used some specialization. These results suggest that, while few schools teach largely by specialization, the use of specialization increases with the age of pupils. The not-maintained schools as a group use more specialization than the maintained schools, particularly with the over-11 group.

Only a very small percentage of schools use mostly team teaching with either the under-11 or the over-11 age groups (2 % and 1 %), the majority for both groups indicating that no team teaching was used (59 % and 61 %).

For the under-11 age group no school relies mainly on group teaching and only 11 % do so for the over-11 group. The large majority of schools use a combination of individual and group teaching for both age groups (70 % and 72 %).

The methods of teaching used in the special classes and units are similar to those for the special schools. The general pattern is that the older the age range being catered for, the greater the likelihood of specialization. Classes and units using mostly team teaching are rare, as are those using only group teaching. In a later open-ended question, which asked classes and units to say in what ways their methods of teaching differed from those of pupils' parent schools, over 90 % of those who responded (65 % of all C/Us) stated that they had a greater degree of individualized teaching than parent schools and over 20 % mentioned greater flexibility in timetabling.

ALLOCATION TO GROUPS

Special schools were asked to rank five criteria in order of importance in allocating pupils to teaching groups, rank 5 being used for the most important. The median and means for the five criteria are shown in Table 5.3. Here again we find evidence of the overriding importance of teacher pupil relationships in the treatment of maladjusted children, 44 % of schools ranking teacher pupil compatibility as the most important criterion in allocating pupils to groups. Family grouping, on the other hand, was ranked highest by only 8 % of schools.

Table 5.3 Importance of criteria in allocating pupils to teching groups (Q18)

	Median	Mean
A compatible teacher/pupil group	4·3	3·7
A compatible peer group	3·8	3·3
Group of similar educational attainment	2·9	2·8
A group of similar ages	2·9	2·7
Family group with a wide age range	1·3	1·6

REMEDIAL PROVISION

With 68 % of pupils estimated as needing remedial education in the basic skills and 64 % perceived as seriously or very seriously underachieving on entry to the schools in relation to their potential, remedial teaching can be expected to play a prominent part in the educational programme of most of the schools. And indeed it does so. Eighty-five per cent of all the schools make remedial teaching part of normal classroom work, more than one half of these (58 %) also making it a specialist provision. Only 11 % of schools make remedial teaching a specialist provision only—that is, not as part of normal classwork. These results strongly suggest that much of the teaching of fundamental skills, which takes up more than one third of classwork time, has a remedial purpose for the greater proportion of pupils.

In 88 % of the special classes and units, like the special schools, remedial teaching is part of classroom work. Thirty-eight per cent make it a specialist provision and 26 % have such a provision available in the parent schools and use it.

NON-ACADEMIC OUTCOMES OF EDUCATIONAL ACTIVITIES

All teachers know that any educational activity has outcomes, planned or otherwise, other than those that might be classed as purely academic. The special schools were asked to say which educational activities provide the best opportunities of working towards nine pre-specified outcomes that might be considered important, possibly essential, in the treatment of maladjustment. The question was in open-ended form and the coding frames adopted were evolved from the responses. Twenty-three schools failed to respond and two responded 'all subjects' for all the outcomes and were excluded from the analysis. Of the remaining eighty-nine schools, six responded for 3 or less outcomes, four responded for 4, 5 or 6, and seventy-nine responded for 7 or more. Table 5.4 shows each of the outcomes with the educational activities ranked according to the number of nominations they received and that number expressed as a percentage of the total number of nominations for that outcome. Only the top three ranked are shown unless the percentage of nominations of the third ranked does not exceed the fourth ranked by more than 5 % in which case the fourth ranked is also shown.

The table shows that in general the subjects making up the core curriculum of the special schools are viewed by the schools as providing the best opportunities of working towards outcomes which might be thought to contribute to a successful treatment of maladjustment. Fundamental skills, which are allocated more than one third of classwork time, are seen to provide good opportunities of working towards *enhanced self-respect* and *a sense of achievement*, both of which seem closely associated with an improvement of self-image through success which featured so prominently in the treatments thought best to achieve personal, social or educational re-adjustment (see Chapter 4). Arts and crafts (including handicrafts) and P.E., games and allied subjects, which between them also account for more than one third of classwork time, are also thought to have therapeutic qualities. Together they account for more than one half of all the nominations for four of the outcomes, *ability to co-operate*, *self-control*, *enjoyment* and *relief of tension*, and nearly one half for *a sense of achievement*. P.E., games and allied subjects is clearly ranked first for *consideration for others* and Arts and crafts (incl. handicrafts) marginally so for *insight into personal/emotional problems*.

Drama and music, which are not so widely taught in schools, attain some of the higher rankings here. Drama appears five times in Table 5.4 and music twice. It may well be that they are taught in only 70 % of schools because of difficulties in obtaining staff able to teach them effectively rather than because of adverse opinion of their therapeutic qualities.

The lowest consensus of opinion regarding educational activities that

Table 5.4　Non-academic outcomes of educational activities (Q23)

Outcome	No. of nominations	% of total nominations	Educational activities
Ability to co-operate *(n = 126)	51	40	P.E., games and allied subjects
	20	16	Arts and crafts (incl. handicrafts)
	19	15	Drama
Enhanced self-respect (n = 95)	43	45	Fundamental skills/basic subjects
	25	26	P.E., games and allied subjects
	14	15	Arts and crafts (incl. handicrafts)
Insight into personal/ emotional problems (n = 108)	20	19	Arts and crafts (incl. handicrafts)
	19	18	Discussion
	15	14	Humanities and religious education
	13	12	Drama
Relief of tension (n = 157)	49	31	Arts and crafts (incl. handicrafts)
	44	28	P.E., games and allied subjects
	21	13	Drama
	14	9	Music
Enjoyment (n = 46)	48	33	Arts and crafts (incl. handicrafts)
	38	26	P.E., games and allied subjects
	17	12	Music
	11	8	Drama
Understanding of human relations (n = 84)	26	31	Humanities and religious education
	11	13	Discussion
	10	12	Stories and literature

Table 5.4 *Contd*

Outcome	No. of nominations	% of total nominations	Educational activities
Self-control (*n* = 106)	43	41	P.E., games and allied subjects
	23	22	Arts and crafts (incl. handicrafts)
	10	9	Fundamental skills/basic subjects
	7	7	Drama
Consideration for others (*n* = 80)	19	24	P.E., games and allied subjects
	11	14	Humanities and religious education
	6	8	Arts and crafts (incl. handicrafts)
	5	6	Social studies
A sense of achievement (*n* = 95)	32	34	Arts and crafts (incl. handicrafts)
	26	27	Fundamental skills/basic subjects
	14	15	P.E., games and allied subjects

* *n* = total number of nominations.

provide the best opportunities of working towards the given outcomes was for the outcome *insight into personal/emotional problems*. No activity attained 20 % of the nominations and less than 5 % separates the first three ranks.

OUTSIDE VISITS AND LEISURE ACTIVITIES

Nearly all of the schools (98 %) make use of outside visits. Although schools were asked to indicate if the visits were 'primarily' *extensions of classwork, part of social training*, or *for pleasure and reward*, 42 % indicated all three. The remaining responses were fairly equally distributed between three.

Leisure activities, both inside and outside of the schools are too many and various to catalogue usefully, a point made by two respondents who— perhaps summing up the real situation—responded: 'a wide variety of activities used allowing for waves of interest and fall off so that a constant flow of items is necessary' and 'a wide range varying according to inclination and season'. What is of particular interest however, especially as we are referring to 'maladjusted' pupils, is that many schools mentioned pupil membership of various outside organizations such as youth clubs; army, naval, St. John's Ambulance or Red Cross cadets, and scouts, guides, brownies or cubs. It is also of interest that some 96 % of schools responded to this question (Q23) which is possibly an indication of the importance the schools attach to providing, or enabling access to, leisure activities for which, as was shown in Chapter 4, boarding schools allow over 4½ hours in a typical day and day schools nearly 2 hours.

USEFUL BOOKS, MATERIALS, AIDS AND EQUIPMENT

Nearly one third of the schools did not respond to question 29 which asked which children's books, materials, aids and equipment they have found particularly useful in the teaching of maladjusted pupils and a further 8 % made only a general comment. Moreover the responses that were made were, as with leisure activities, many and various with no individual item standing out from the rest in terms of number of times mentioned. For books, more were concerned with remedial reading than with any other individual subject, most of the well known remedial and other reading schemes being mentioned—so here again we find evidence of the importance of remedial work within these schools. For materials, aids and equipment many again were concerned with the basic subjects. The overall impression is that books, materials, aids and equipment generally found useful for teaching pupils in ordinary schools, particularly those requiring remedial help, are also useful in teaching maladjusted pupils, with no particular items being generally recognized as particularly useful.

ASSESSMENT AND RECORDING OF PROGRESS

Only 10 % of the schools have no regular schedule for the assessment and recording of pupils' educational progress, these schools doing this work as occasion arises. More than one half of all schools (53 %) assess and record educational progress each term, 36 % of these in conjunction with *as occasion arises*. Eighteen per cent of all schools assess and record monthly or less (26 % of these in conjunction with *as occasion arises*), the remaining 19 % of schools assessing and recording annually with 42 % of these doing this work also *as occasion arises*. Overall, the assessment and recording of educational progress is less frequent but more regularized than it is for pupils' personal/social progress (see Chapter 4).

In 47 % of schools only the teaching staff contribute to the assessment and recording of educational progress. Child care staff also contribute in 35 % of schools, two-thirds of these contributing in a full team meeting as a quarter of schools use full team meetings—that is, teaching, child care, and specialist team staff—to assess and record educational progress. To assist in this assessment 47% of schools use some standardized measure or measures.

Around one half of all C/Us use standard IQ and attainment tests during the selection of pupils, and during a pupil's attendance. Slightly less than one third however use these for assessment immediately prior to re-entry to the ordinary school system. Units, attached or autonomous, tend to use such tests more than special classes.

SUMMARY

For most special schools and C/Us for disturbed pupils English language, Mathematics, Arts and crafts and P.E. and allied subjects—supported by one or more of the humanity subjects—make up what might be called their 'core curriculum'. In the special schools these subjects between them take up over three quarters of available classwork time, with fundamental skills alone taking up over one third of that time. As the great majority of special schools and C/Us make remedial education a normal part of classroom work, much of the work covered by fundamental skills will be remedial. In addition to their more directly educational qualities, these core subjects are seen by the special schools to have therapeutic values, particularly Arts and crafts and P.E. and allied subjects.

The teaching methods used in the special schools are generally a combination of individual and group teaching with some specialization, particularly in the senior schools. Team teaching methods are extremely rare. In the allocation of pupils to teaching groups teacher/pupil and pupil/pupil compatibility are widely considered to be more important than the educational attainment or age of pupils.

6 Outcomes and evidence of success

The aim of the project, with which this report has been concerned, was given in the Introduction as 'to investigate successful practice in the educational treatment of disturbed pupils'. Many problems, however, centre on this notion of successful practice. We can ask, for example, successful in whose terms? For those of the school, the LEA, the child or his family, or perhaps even those of society in general? We can ask how 'successful practice' in the schools to be recognized and possibly measured? Is it to be by the amelioration of symptoms for which a pupil is referred to the school or those he exhibits on placement for, as Williams (1962) points out, the two are often very different? Or is to be by the number of pupils returned back to the ordinary school system? Or perhaps, in view of the case histories of many of these pupils, simply in the number of pupils it can contain without having to resort to exclusion? Or does the evidence have to lie in the life led by a pupil after he has left school rather than in his life within the school? And is an apparent recovery due to the work of the school or spontaneous remission?

The questions, the problems, are endless but nevertheless an attempt at some sort of assessment of success seems necessary in an 'investigation of successful practice'. In recognition of the many problems surrounding this area the question of how the schools themselves measure their success was put somewhat indirectly and cautiously. The schools were simply given the opportunity to mention any evidence of the success of their work gained from follow-up studies, re-assessments, examination results, sporting achievements or anything else (Q45).

Over 40% of the schools either offered no evidence or made a meaningless comment like 'a good deal' (33%) or stated that it was impossible to assess or that they were reluctant to offer evidence (10%) for various reasons, for example, that the 'yardstick must be the sort of marriage and family produced'. All but 12% of the responses of the remaining schools fall into three categories or combination thereof: return to normal school or on to employment; achievements in the academic field; and recognizable achievements in non-academic fields. More than one half of these schools specified return to normal school or on to employment (62 %), mostly in conjunction with one or both of the other two categories. Again, more than one half (53 %) mentioned academic achievements, also mostly in conjunction with one or both of the other two categories. The responses that could not be encompassed by these three categories mentioned such things as 'frequent return of ex-pupils to visit', 'happy marriages', 'leading happy worthwhile lives' and 'no problems with police or need for psychiatric help' as evidence of their success.

OUTCOMES FOR PUPILS

The outcomes for pupils leaving the schools were investigated in questions 41 and 42. In the view of the small number of pupils attending the schools and hence the predictably small number of pupils that might leave in any one year, a two-year period, between September 1973 and August 1975, was used. Question 41 was concerned with those pupils who had left the schools below the statutory leaving age (16 years) in this period and question 42 with those who left at or after the statutory age. Table 6.1 shows these data.

During the specified two-year period 1346 pupils left the schools below the statutory leaving age and a further 1077 left at or above the statutory age, making a total of 2423 pupils. (Note: 174 pupils remained within the schools beyond the statutory leaving age and therefore these are not included in the total number of pupils leaving.) This total number represents around one half of the pupils who could be expected to be attending those schools that responded, which implies an annual leaving rate of around 25 %. This in turn suggests that the mean length of stay of pupils attending schools for the maladjusted is around four years.

More than one half (56 %) of the pupils who left during the two-year period left before reaching the statutory leaving age. Of these leavers 59 % were transferred in accordance with the school's recommendation to ordinary schools or to special schools other than those for the maladjusted. This strongly suggests that, in the opinion of those making the recommendations, more than one half of the pupils who leave below the statutory leaving age leave with maladjustment either no longer recognized as being a handicap to them or as being their predominant handicap. Of those who left at or above the statutory leaving age only 18 % left without employment at the point of leaving or went on to other specialist provision. And of the total number of pupils who left during the period only 5 % were excluded from the schools.

If success is defined in terms of the containment of pupils, the data show that the schools are undoubtedly successful. If we define success according

Table 6.1 Outcomes for pupils leaving the schools between September 1973 and August 1975 (Q41 & 42)

(a) Leaving below statutory age (n of schools = 103)

Number of pupils who were	Withdrawn by parents	Excluded	After being recommended for transfer	TOTALS
Transferred to other schools for emotional or behavioural difficulties	20	44	167	231
Transferred to other special schools	29	14	158	201
Transferred to ordinary schools	104	22	642	768
Otherwise provided for	42	33	71	146
TOTALS	195	113	1038	1346

(b) Leaving above statutory age (n of schools = 80)

Number of pupils who				TOTALS
Remained on the roll of the school				174
Left with employment found at point of leaving				708
Left without employment found at point of leaving				159
Left to attend college of F.E. for non-examination work				41
Left to attend college of F.E. for examination work				116
Left to increase examination passes				13
Left for admission to other specialist provisions				40
TOTALS				1251
				2597*

* 174 remained at school, thus 2423 actually left

to criteria of success suggested by most of the schools responding to question 45 then the following outcomes could be taken as indicators of success: transferred to ordinary school after recommendation; left with employment at point of leaving; left to attend college for examination work, and left to increase examination passes. These indicants represent 1479 pupils, 61 % of all pupils leaving the schools in the two-year period. According to these, perhaps simplistic, criteria of success then it could be claimed that the practices within the schools for the maladjusted are largely successful.

For the group leaving below the statutory age, the all-age range schools had proportionately more of these pupils (58 %) transferred to ordinary schools after recommendation than did the primary schools (43 %) which tended to have proportionately more of these pupils transferred after recommendation to other schools for the maladjusted (21 %) or other special schools (22 %) than did the all-age range schools (11 % and 12 % respectively). Fifty-six per cent of pupils leaving day schools below the statutory age went on to ordinary schools after recommendation, compared to 42 % of those leaving the boarding schools below the statutory age. Similarly, 18 % of those leaving day schools below the statutory age went on to other special schools (not for the maladjusted) compared to 12 % for the boarding schools. Care should be exercised in extrapolating freely from these findings. Differences in outcomes for the pupils may be an artifact of differing populations of pupils rather than of the efficacy of the schools for, even where we found no significant differences in the distribution of the types of disorders with schools (see Chapter 2), the severity of the symptoms displayed by pupils was not investigated.

PREDOMINANT PATTERNS OF BEHAVIOUR AND OUTCOMES

Correlation coefficients were computed for the percentage of pupils estimated as falling within each of the categories of predominant behaviour pattern used in question 9 and the number of pupils under statutory leaving age going on to other placements by recommendation. Great· caution, however, must be exercised in any interpretation of these results; they should be regarded as possible generators of hypotheses rather than as supporters of hypotheses. It must be clearly understood that, while the estimates of the predominant patterns of behaviour referred to pupils who were currently attending the schools, the data regarding placement outcomes referred to pupils who had left the schools. Moreover, these data should be seen as referring to schools and not to individual children. Nevertheless, in so far as the distribution of the various types of disorder— or the perceived distribution—within the schools remains stable over time, these coefficients may be of interest.

The coefficients that were significant at or beyond the 5 % probability level using a two-tail test are shown in Table 6.2. Schools that responded zero for either of the two variables in question were omitted from the particular analysis. (In Table 6.2 n = number of schools included in the analysis.) What is most noticeable about the coefficients shown is that they involve what many would regard as the most difficult disorders to treat successfully, particularly the psychotic child, and that none has 'recommended transfer to ordinary schools' as one of the variables.

Table 6.2   Correlation coefficients for predominant patterns of behaviour and recommended outcomes for those leaving below the statutory age (Q9 & 41)

Predominant pattern of behaviour and recommended transfer	r	p
Developmental disorder (n = 68)		
To other schools for emotional or behavioural difficulties	0·28	⩽0·05
To provisions other than special or ordinary schools	0·30	⩽0·01
Psychosis (n = 49)		
To other schools for emotional or behavioural difficulties	0·33	⩽0·05
To other special schools	0·50	⩽0·001
To provisions other than special or ordinary schools	0·43	⩽0·01
Personality disorders (n = 50)		
To other special schools	0·34	⩽0·01

DURATION OF ATTENDANCE IN CLASSES AND UNITS

There is a tremendous range of differences in the periods of time pupils attend C/Us (see Table 6.3). As few C/Us (16 %) plan at the time of a pupil's admission what the duration of attendance will be, the explanation of this tremendous range does not lie in differences in predetermined planning policies.

This notion is further supported by the data shown in Table 6.4 which show significant differences in duration of pupil's attendance (all p< 0·01) in C/Us of different type of age range, although no differences in planning at time of admittance were found for these. None of the differences in duration of pupils' attendance for C/Us with different pupil attendance bases were significant although those catering only for pupils attending part time were least likely to plan the duration of a pupil's attendance at the time of admission (PT C/Us = 7 %, FT = 17 %, FT/PT 15 %).

Table 6.3 Duration of attendance at classes and units (in school months)*

n of C/Us	Duration	Mean	Median	Min-max
156	Shortest duration for a given pupil	3·7	2·4	1–18
155	Longest duration for a given pupil	25·8	25·7	2–67
144	Most usual duration for most pupils	13·5	12·6	1–40

* 9 school months = 1 calendar year

The data from the autonomous units suggest that, while most of their pupils attend the unit for just over one year, most have a minority of pupils who have attended for around three years.

Attached units have much longer periods for all the three durations of attendance than either the classes or autonomous units, while the classes have shorter periods than either the autonomous or attached units for all three durations. There is almost certainly a relationship between the relatively large units and the other two types of provision and the similarly large and consistent differences existing between the primary and the other age range C/Us. As may be remembered from Chapter 1, 81 % of the attached units are for primary age ranges only, while 60 % of primary age

Table 6.4 Mean durations of attendance for type, age range and attendance basis of C/U (in school months)

C/U	Duration shortest	longest	most usual
Type			
Autonomous unit	3·0	27·3	11·5
Attached unit	5·6	29·8	18·8
Special class	2·8	7·9	10·5
Age range			
Junior	5·5	31·0	17·6
Senior	2·3	18·8	10·0
All age	2·0	26·4	8·8
Attendance basis			
Full time only	4·2	27·9	14·5
Part time only	2·7	24·5	13·0
Full and part time	3·5	22·9	12·0

C/Us are attached units. Any attempt to explain these differences in Table 6.4 must therefore take this relationship between age range and attached units into account. The longer durations of attendance for attached units and junior age C/Us, which again in Chapter 1 (Table 1.3) were shown predominantly to accept pupils on a full-time attendance basis only, are not reflected in the data in Table 6.4 relating to the attendance basis of the C/U. The table strongly suggests therefore that the age range of pupils catered for, or the type of C/U, has a greater influence than a pupil's attendance being either full or part time on the duration of his attendance.

A full matrix of correlation coefficients was computed for the three predominant patterns of behaviour and educational problems of pupils and duration of attendance data. Two-tailed tests of significance were used and those attaining significance at or beyond the 0·05 level were as follows:

Outgoing behaviour and longest duration	$r = -0.17$ ($p<0.05$)
Neither pattern predominant and longest duration	$r = 0.18$ ($p<0.05$)
Neither pattern predominant and usual duration	$r = 0.18$ ($p<0.05$)
No special educational problems and shortest duration	$r = -0.25$ ($p<0.01$)
No special educational problems and shortest duration	$r = -0.25$ ($p<0.01$)
No special educational problems and longest duration	$r = -0.22$ ($p<0.01$)
No special educational problems and usual duration	$r = -0.23$ ($p<0.01$)

The caveats for other coefficients given earlier in this report also apply here, the main one being that the two variables do not necessarily refer to the same groups of children. It should also be noted that the smallest n involved was 140 thus enabling statistical significance to be attained by quite low coefficients. Nevertheless, those referring to no special educational problems and duration of attendance are most interesting. Firstly, they are remarkably consistent and secondly, they do attain a high level of significance. The negative coefficients indicate that the more pupils without any special educational problems a C/U has then the shorter its shortest, longest, and most usual duration of pupil attendance is likely to be.

FEATURES CONTRIBUTING TO SUCCESS IN THE ORDINARY SCHOOL

The questionnaire to schools other than special schools for the maladjusted (QB) asked recipients to weight certain features, using a five-point scale (5 = most important), according to their contribution to the school's success with disturbed children. These features and the median and mean weightings they received are shown in Table 6.5. The general climate of a school, whatever this embodies, was seen as the most important contributory feature to a school's success in this respect. Those schools which have a special class or unit for disturbed pupils see the availability of this specific provision as a most important contributory feature to their success. The relatively low weightings allocated to *emphasis on educational progress* as contributing towards their success with disturbed pupils is of particular interest in view of the importance attached to scholastic progress in the special schools.

Table 6.5   Median and mean weighting of features contributing to a school's success with disturbed pupils

Feature	Median	Mean
General school climate	4·7	4·5
Specific provision for disturbed pupils*	4·6	4·0
Quality of pastoral care	4·3	3·9
Skill in the management of disruptive pupils	3·9	3·8
Staff understanding of emotional disturbance	3·9	3·8
Emphasis on educational progress	2·7	2·6
Supportive services for the staff	2·4	2·5

* Only schools with a special class or attached unit included

SUMMARY

Many schools for the maladjusted see some evidence of the success of their work in the number of pupils who return to the ordinary school system or go on to employment, and in recognizable attainments in both academic and non-academic fields. Around 25 % of pupils leave the schools each year, more than one half of these below the statutory leaving age. The majority of those leaving below the statutory age either return to the ordinary school system or go on to special schools other than those for the maladjusted. Of those leaving at or beyond the statutory age over 80 % went on either to employment or to colleges for further education.

There is a wide range of differences in length of pupils' attendance at C/Us, and the data suggest that these differences are not related to whether a C/U accepts pupils only a full-time or part-time basis.

7 Overview

In Chapter 4 two features of, or approaches to, the treatment of disturbed pupils in special schools for the maladjusted clearly stand out, both in terms of their widespread use and in their perceived efficacy. The first of these is concerned with *the quality and nature of interpersonal relationships* and the second is concerned with *improvement of pupil self-image through success.* Once identified, supportive evidence for the almost overriding importance of these two features can be found throughout the data. For interpersonal relationships, schools see that it is important that these are warm, caring, accepting and, where possible, have continuity. The small size of the schools and teacher/pupil ratios of around 1:7 can be viewed as facilitators of the development and demonstration of warm, caring and accepting attitudes on the part of staff. In the allocation of pupils to teaching groups the most important criteria are, almost universally among the schools, teacher/pupil and pupil/peer relationships. Adult/pupil relationships, often expressed as approval or disapproval, pleasure or displeasure, are seen to play a large part in the management of pupils. And finally, as if to underline all this, it is the personal qualities of staff rather than specific training that are generally regarded as most valuable in staff working with disturbed children.

The importance of improving the self-image of pupils through success strongly suggests that, for many of these pupils, their experience of failure has been frequent and damaging. This notion is strongly supported by the data. All but 8% of pupils in special schools are estimated to have been underachieving in relation to their potential on entry, and two-thirds require specific remedial help. Almost all the schools make provision for remedial work, the very great majority making it a normal part of classroom work. Furthermore, the teaching of fundamental skills, which takes up more than one third of classwork time, is seen by many schools as providing good opportunities for working towards enhanced self-respect and a sense of achievement for pupils. Also, the use of approval and praise in the management of pupils must play a part in developing a pupil's awareness of his successes in both the educational and social life of the school.

These two features then are seen to be beneficial to all types of disturbance and are incorporated into the total programme of almost all schools. The remainder of a school's programme will be related to, and possibly influenced to some extent by, its particular group of pupils. It is reasonable to extrapolate from the data that the more conduct disorder pupils a school has, the more likely it is to stress such things as routine, discipline and overall structure. The more neurotic disorder pupils in a school the more likely it is to stress what might be called the 'bringing-out techniques', such as freedom to express feelings and opportunities for regression. But the widespread prevalence in the schools of pupils showing symptoms associated with conduct disorder, and possibly the nature and degree of the problems they present, is evidenced in the orientation of the total programmes of most schools towards those treatments widely thought to be effective for the conduct disorder group rather than towards those for the neurotic disorder group. Finally, irrespective of the disorder group or orientation that predominates within a school, most see the provision of a varied and stimulating educational programme as being beneficial for most disturbed pupils, and scholastic progress as an important ingredient in the running of a community for disturbed pupils; recognizable educational achievements were mentioned by a majority of those schools which gave evidence of success in their work.

However, apart from the emphasis on remedial help, there is little in the information from the questionnaire to distinguish educational practice with disturbed pupils from what might be considered good educational practice with any pupil. It includes both group and individual teaching, with some specialization in certain areas. The core subjects of the curriculum, which take up over two-thirds of classwork time, are fundamental skills, Arts and crafts and P.E. and allied subjects, which are thought by many to have therapeutic effects in addition to their more obvious or more direct outcomes.

The importance of the adults who are concerned and involved also stands out clearly throughout, not only in the part they play in the all-important development and maintenance of close, understanding relationships, but in all spheres of the work. In such small schools they work, and often live, in close proximity with the children and each other, so that staff disharmony inevitably must have an adverse effect upon a community for disturbed pupils. The majority of schools take direct action, often through discussion, to create an atmosphere of shared responsibility and friendship among the staff. Also through discussion, staff support each other and share ideas, knowledge, experience and decision making—and their discussion does not stop at the staff room door. Discussion with pupils both individually and in groups, is widely used and thought both important and effective. As Bridgeland (1971) puts it so admirably, 'In few other spheres of work is the individual person so important, so essential, so central'.

There are some interesting similarities and differences between the work in special classes and units for disturbed pupils and that in special schools for the maladjusted. Unlike the special schools, C/Us overwhelmingly operate on a daily attendance basis only, with over one half accepting part-time pupils. Nearly one half of C/Us accept only pupils below the age of twelve years, whereas only 15% of special schools do so. However, provisions catering for pupils across the full school age range are far less widespread among C/Us than they are among the special schools. Like the special schools, the C/Us have low teacher/pupil ratios, around 1:6/8 according to the type of provision. The majority of pupils attending the C/Us, as in the special schools, display features of behaviour associated with the conduct disorder category, some in conjunction with features associated with the neurotic disorder group. As in the special schools, boys outnumber the girls in the C/Us but only in a ratio of about 2:1, whereas the ratio in special schools was about 5:1. Also, as in the special schools, with few pupils having no educational problems and most requiring remedial help in the basic subjects, the great majority of C/Us make remedial teaching part of normal classwork. The methods of teaching used also resemble those found in the special schools, including both individual and group teaching with little specialization. The main core subjects are the same as those found within the special schools, but the C/Us generally offer a narrower range of subjects than do the special schools. The C/Us, perhaps more so than the special schools, see members of the specialist team—particularly the psychologist—as a valuable source of support for staff. Finally, the average length of pupil attendance in the C/Us is slightly more than eighteen calendar months, apparently a shorter average period than in the special schools.

In closing this report there seems to be little need to suggest areas for further and possibly fruitful research. Such areas suggest themselves throughout the report and, such are the frailties of data collection by questionnaire, that, to a certain extent, almost every finding needs further investigation. While the report, like most of its kind, raises more questions than it answers, it nevertheless largely confirms, rather than contradicts, both the views expressed in most of the recent literature (see Laslett, 1977) and the common knowledge of those working in the schools. To add support and possibly validity to what is already known and to provide data which provoke discussion, interest and possibly new questions, is always a worthwhile exercise. If this report has gone any way towards doing this the project team will be well satisfied.

Appendix A
Selection and response to questionnaires of schools other than for the maladjusted and special classes and units

In the spring of 1975 a letter was sent to every LEA in England and Wales asking them to nominate schools or special classes 'where good work with disturbed pupils is going on'. A total of 550 schools, classes and units were nominated and in the spring of 1976 these were each sent two questionnaires: the first, QB, to be completed by schools and the other, QC, to be completed, where appropriate, by teachers in charge of special classes or units for disturbed pupils. (Ten community homes providing full-time education were nominated but were not included in the survey.)

The questionnaires were returned as follows:

  174 returned QB completed
   84 returned QC completed
   89 returned both QB and QC completed.

Of the 263 questionnaires (QB) returned by schools, 105 (40%) were returned by special schools other than for the maladjusted and, of these, one half were special schools for the educationally subnormal. Special schools were omitted from the analysis contained in this report.

It must be emphasized that the method of selecting recipients of questionnaires B and C negates any claim that respondents are necessarily a fair representation of either ordinary schools or special classes or units at large.

The return of QC by the type of special class or unit is reported in Chapter 1.

Appendix B
Questionnaire to special schools for the maladjusted (QA)

SCHOOLS COUNCIL PROJECT: EDUCATION OF DISTURBED PUPILS

PHILIPPA FAWCETT COLLEGE, LONDON

School ....

Head teacher ....

Address ....

Maintaining authority ....

How long has the school been open with
its present functions?   [   ]   Years

ADMINISTRATION

1. Type of school—Please tick in appropriate circle

○ *a. Boarding school*
○ *b. Day school*
○ *c. Boarding/Day school*

○ *a. Maintained special school for maladjusted pupils*
○ *b. Non-maintained special school for maladjusted pupils*
○ *c. Independent school taking only maladjusted pupils*

2.   Number of pupils on roll in January, 1976

	Boys
	Girls
	Total

3.   Mixed boarding/day schools only, number in residence

	Boys
	Girls
	Total

4.   Age range of pupils

from [   ] *years to* [   ] *years*

STAFFING

5.   Numbers when fully staffed:

	Full time	Part time	P-T expressed as F-T equivalent
Teaching staff			
Child care			
Ancillary staff			

Please give details of ancillary staff members, e.g. duties, titles, and level of involvement with the children.

6.   Which of the following members of a specialist team is available outside and inside the school?

	Inside	Approx. no. sess. p.w.	Outside	Approx. no. sess. p.w.
Psychologist	◯		◯	
Psychiatrist	◯		◯	
Psychotherapist	◯		◯	
School social worker	◯		◯	
Other specialist staff	◯		◯	

Please specify other specialist staff

INFORMATION ABOUT PUPILS

7. Estimated range of pupils' intelligence

% *Very much below average* *(I.Q. below 70)*

% *Below average* *(I.Q. 70–84)*

% *Average (low)* *(I.Q. 85–99)*

% *Average (high)* *(I.Q. 100–114)*

% *Above average* *(I.Q. 115–129)*

% *Very much above average* *(I.Q. above 130)*

100% *TOTAL*

8. Pupil achievement levels on entry in relation to potential

% *Not underachieving*

% *Slightly underachieving*

% *Seriously underachieving*

% *Very seriously underachieving*

100% *TOTAL*

PREDOMINANT PATTERNS OF BEHAVIOUR

9. We recognise the reluctance of some colleagues to classify children according to the predominant patterns of their behaviour but we should be greatly helped by this information. For this purpose no child should be counted twice.

☐ % *CONDUCT DISORDERS:*
(socially unacceptable behaviour such as aggression, destructiveness, stealing, lying, truanting, etc.)

☐ % *NEUROTIC DISORDERS:*
(excessive anxiety, depression, isolation, phobia, tics, etc.)

☐ % *MIXED CONDUCT AND NEUROTIC DISORDERS:*
(both present, neither predominant)

☐ % *DEVELOPMENTAL DISORDERS:*
(general immaturity, enuresis, encopresis, language disorder not secondary to other disturbances, etc.)

☐ % *PSYCHOSIS:*
(severe disintegration of behaviour involving loss of contact with reality)

☐ % *PERSONALITY DISORDERS:*
(fixed abnormalities of personality that cannot be included in any other category)

☐ % *NEUROLOGICAL ABNORMALITIES:*
(Pupils with clinical evidence of brain injury, epilepsy, minimal cerebral dysfunction, etc.)

☐   % *EDUCATIONAL DIFFICULTIES:*
(not secondary to subnormality nor maladjustment)

☐   % *OTHERS*   *Please specify*

METHODS

10. The aim of special education for maladjusted children as defined in the *Handicapped pupils and Special Education Regulations* is to effect 'their personal, social, or educational re-adjustment'. Below are a number of methods which have been thought to be effective in achieving this aim. Please tick those used with your pupils.

CODE

1 ○ A varied and stimulating educational programme

2 ○ Warm caring attitudes in adult to child relationships

3 ○ Programmed learning

4 ○ Systematic use of incentives or deterrents

5 ○ Shared responsibility

6 ○ Drug treatment

7 ○ Remedial teaching in the basic skills

8 ○ Creative work in the arts

CODE

9 ○ Individual psychotherapy (under direction of trained therapist)

10 ○ Techniques of classroom management derived from learning theory

11 ○ Improvement of self-image through success

12 ○ Opportunity for regression

13 ○ Opportunity for shared activities with other children

14 ○ Unconditional affection

CODE

CODE

15 ◯ Behaviour therapy with individual pupils (under the direction of a psychologist)

16 ◯ Group therapy (under direction of trained therapist)

17 ◯ Individual counselling and discussion

18 ◯ Freedom to express feelings

19 ◯ Continuity of child/adult relationships

20 ◯ Teaching of social skills

21 ◯ Group discussion (with teacher or child care staff)

22 ◯ Firm consistent discipline

Which have you found most effective in relation to the different types of disorder? You may select six for each type, entering the code number in the boxes.

Conduct disorders:						
Neurotic disorders:						
Mixed conduct and neurotic disorders:						
Developmental disorders:						
Psychosis:						
Personality disorders:						
Neurological abnormalities:						
Educational difficulties:						
All disturbed children:						

11. In running a community for disturbed pupils, which of the following have you found most important? You are asked to weight these items according to the scale below. (Please note that weighting may be used more than once.)

Most important   5

Very important   4

Important   3

Less important   2

Least important   1

☐	*Pupil involvement in management*
☐	*Scholastic progress*
☐	*Gaining of insight (pupil)*
☐	*Accepting relationships*
☐	*Expressive work in the arts*
☐	*Opportunities for regression*
☐	*Routine and discipline*

ENVIRONMENTAL TREATMENT

12.   Indicate how much time in a typical day is spent on the following, and to what degree pupils are free to participate or not.

	Hours	Free choice	Limited choice	No choice
1. School work in the classroom	☐	○	○	○
2. Organised leisure activities	☐	○	○	○
3. Free leisure activities	☐	○	○	○
4. Meals and snacks	☐	○	○	○
5. Personal physical care	☐	○	○	○
6. Communal living duties	☐	○	○	○
TOTAL	☐			

13. In what practical ways, if any, do you make use of the following to further the pupil's emotional well-being?

> *1. Personal possessions*

> *2. Care of surroundings*

> *3. Routine physical care*

> *4. Minor illness and ailments*

> *5. Going to bed*

> *6. Clothing*

> *7. Meal times*

> *8. Getting up*

For boarding schools

14. Please describe how you use your staff for the care of pupils outside of school hours.

15. What incentives and deterrents, if any, have you found most effective in the management of pupils showing the following predominant types of disorder?

	incentives	deterrents
Conduct disorders	1. 2. 3.	1. 2. 3.
Neurotic disorders	1. 2. 3.	1. 2. 3.
Mixed conduct/ neurotic disorders	1. 2. 3.	1. 2. 3.
Developmental disorders	1. 2. 3.	1. 2. 3.
Psychosis	1. 2. 3.	1. 2. 3.
Personality disorders	1. 2. 3.	1. 2. 3.
Neurological abnormalities	1. 2. 3.	1. 2. 3.
Educational difficulties	1. 2. 3.	1. 2. 3.
All disturbed children	1. 2. 3.	1. 2. 3.

16. In what ways, formal and informal, do pupils participate in:

> 1. The running of the community?

> 2. Their own treatment programme?

MEDICAL AND PSYCHOLOGICAL TREATMENT

17. What total percentage of pupils, within and outside the school, have

☐ % Individual psychotherapy?

☐ % Group psychotherapy?

☐ % Behaviour therapy?

☐ % Drug treatment?

EDUCATIONAL TREATMENT

18. Please rank the following criteria in order of importance in allocating pupils to teaching groups. (Rank 5 = most important, 1 = least important)

☐ *A group of similar ages*

☐ *Family group with a wide age range*

☐ *Group of similar educational attainment*

☐	*A compatible peer group*
☐	*A compatible teacher/pupil group*

19. How is the teaching in the school organised?
    Tick column (a) for pupils under 11 years, and (b) for older pupils:

	(a)	(b)	
1.	○	○	*No specialisation*
2.	○	○	*Some specialisation*
3.	○	○	*Largely specialisation*
1.	○	○	*No team teaching*
2.	○	○	*Some team teaching*
3.	○	○	*Mostly team teaching*
1.	○	○	*Mainly individual teaching*
2.	○	○	*A combination of group/individual work*
3.	○	○	*Mainly class teaching*

20. Which of the subjects below are taught within the school?
    Tick column (a) if the subject is taught in its own right.
    Tick column (b) if the subject is taught as part of an integrated study method:

	(a)	(b)			(a)	(b)	
1.	○	○	*English language*	*7.*	○	○	*Religious or moral education*
2.	○	○	*English literature*				
3.	○	○	*Maths*	*8.*	○	○	*Modern languages*
4.	○	○	*Geography*	*9.*	○	○	*Technical drawing*
5.	○	○	*History*	*10.*	○	○	*Woodwork and or metalwork*
6.	○	○	*Science*				

(a) (b)

11. ◯ ◯ *Music*

12. ◯ ◯ *Arts and crafts*

13. ◯ ◯ *Drama and movement*

14. ◯ ◯ *Domestic subjects*

15. ◯ ◯ *P.E. & allied activities*

16. ◯ ◯ *Careers*

17. ◯ ◯ *Preparation for parenthood*

18. ◯ ◯ *Environmental studies*

19. ◯ ◯ *Commercial subjects*

20. ◯ ◯ *Health education including sex education*

Other subjects taught within the school
Please state method of teaching, i.e. (a) or (b)

---

21. Which additional subjects would you like to introduce into the curriculum?

---

22. Approximately what percentage of 'school' time is generally allocated to the following?

1. [   ] % *P.E. and allied activities*

2. [   ] % *Fundamental skills (reading, writing, maths)*

3. [   ] % *Humanities (literature, history, moral education, etc.)*

4. [   ] % *The sciences*

5. [   ] % *Creative arts (painting, writing, music, drama, etc.)*

6. ⌐‾‾‾‾‾‾¬   % *Handicrafts (wood, metal)*
7. | | % *Others (Pleasure specify.)*
    | 100 % |
    └────────┘   *TOTAL*

23. Please indicate which educational activities have provided the best opportunities of working towards the following:

     1. Ability to co-operate

     2. Enhanced self-respect

     3. Insight into personal/emotional problems

     4. Relief of tension

     5. Enjoyment

     6. Understanding of human relations

     7. Self-control

     8. Consideration for others

     9. A sense of achievement

24. Do you have a plan or programme of activities designed to develop, increase, or practise social skills?

     1. ◯   *YES*   2. ◯   *NO*

     If YES, give details

25. What percentage of your pupils need remedial education in the basic skills?

     ⌐‾‾‾‾‾‾‾¬ %
     └────────┘

26. Is remedial teaching part of the normal classroom work?   ◯ *YES* ◯ *NO*

     Is remedial teaching a specialist provision?   ◯ *YES* ◯ *NO*

27. Do you make use of outside visits?   ◯ *YES* ◯ *NO*

If yes, are the visits <u>primarily</u>
extensions of class work?   ◯

   part of social training?   ◯

   for pleasure and reward?   ◯

28. Please list the leisure activities and occupations available

within the school	outside the school

29. Please name any children's books, teaching materials, aids, and equipment which you have found particularly useful in the teaching of maladjusted pupils.

WORK WITH FAMILIES

30. In which of the following ways is contact between the school and families established and maintained?

		YES	NO
1.	*Contact prior to child's admission*	◯	◯
2.	*Visits for organised events*	◯	◯
3.	*Formal visits to discuss progress*	◯	◯
4.	*Social visits*	◯	◯

5.　　　　*Home visits by social worker*　◯　◯
6.　　　　　　　　*Written reports*　◯　◯
7.　　　　*Group parent meetings*　◯　◯

8.　　　　*Other ways, please specify*　◯　◯

For schools with a school-based social worker

31.　Do the social worker's duties include:

		YES	NO
1.	informing the family about the child's educational progress?	◯	◯
2.	conducting family case-work?	◯	◯
3.	discussion with groups of families?	◯	◯

32.　With which agencies, voluntary and statutory, does the social worker make contact?
Please underline those which have been found to be particularly useful.

THE STAFF

33.　List six personal qualities, including acquired skills, which you would consider most valuable in teachers and child-care staff working with disturbed children.

Teachers	1.
	2.
	3.
	4.
	5.
	6.
Child-care staff	1.
	2.
	3.
	4.
	5.
	6.

34. What ongoing forms of support for staff have you found most valuable?

35. If you have any form of in-service training within the school, please indicate its nature.

36. How do you enable staff of different disciplines to work as a team?

RECORDS AND RESULTS

37. How often is each pupil's progress assessed and recorded?

		Personal/social	*Educational*
1.	*Weekly*	O	O
2.	*Monthly*	O	O
3.	*Termly*	O	O
4.	*Yearly*	O	O
5.	*As occasion arises*	O	O

38. Who contributes to the making of these assessments?

1.	*Teaching staff only*	O	O
2.	*Teaching and child-care staff*	O	O
3.	*Teaching, child-care staff and members of specialist team*	O	O
4.	*Teaching staff and members of specialist team*	O	O
5.	*Head teacher and members of specialist team only*	O	O

39. | What standardised measures, if any, are used in assessing the personal, social or educational readjustment of pupils?

40. | Describe any techniques of assessment and recording devised by the school.

41. How many of your pupils leaving below the statutory age between September 1973 and August 1975 inclusive were:

	Withdrawn by parents	Excluded	After being recommended for transfer
transferred to other schools for emotional or behavioural difficulties?			
transferred to other special schools?			
transferred to ordinary schools?			
Otherwise provided for?			

42.   Of those reaching statutory age how many

remained on the roll of the school?

left with employment found at point of leaving?

left without employment found at point of leaving?

left to attend college of F.E. for non-examination work?

left to attend college of F.E. for examination work?

left to increase examination passes?

left for admission to other specialist provisions?

43.   Specify factors, in any of the following areas, which in your opinion impede the work of the school.

1.   Material resources

2.   Premises and/or situation

3.   *Family influences*

4.   *Staffing*

5.   *Support services*

6.   *Other areas*

44.   Name any books which you and your staff have found particularly useful in relation to your work with disturbed pupils.

45.   You may care to mention here any evidence of the success of your work gained from follow-up studies, reassessments, examination results, sporting achievements, etc.

46. Is there any special feature or aspect of the work in your school which you would like to mention here?

47. We realise that in spite of the length and complexity of this questionnaire you may still feel that you have not had the opportunity to reveal the essence of your philosophy and method. Please use this space for any comments you wish to make, and accept our thanks for your co-operation.

Signed   . . . .

Position   . . . .

Date   . . . .

Other contributors

Appendix C
Questionnaire to special classes and units for disturbed pupils (QC)

SCHOOLS COUNCIL PROJECT: EDUCATION OF DISTURBED PUPILS

PHILIPPA FAWCETT COLLEGE, LONDON

TO BE COMPLETED BY TEACHERS IN CHARGE OF
SPECIAL CLASSES OR UNITS FOR DISTURBED PUPILS

Title of class or unit . . . . Tel: . . .ʌ. . . . .

Name of teacher-in-charge . . . .

Address . . . .

Maintaining authority . . . .

ADMINISTRATION

1. Type of class/unit—please tick in appropriate circles

   ◯ a. autonomous
   ◯ b. administratively part of . . . . school

   ◯ a. caters for pupils solely from parent school
   ◯ b. caters for pupils from more than one school

2. Number of pupils assigned to the class/unit during the week beginning Monday 10th May, 1976:

	Full-time attendance	Part-time attendance
Boys		
Girls		
Total		

Number attending at any one time:

Minimum [   ]   Maximum [   ]

3. Age range of pupils

from [   ] *years to* [   ] *years*

STAFFING

4. Number of staff attached to class/unit

	Teaching	Other
Full-time		
Part-time 50% or above		
Part-time below 50%		

PURPOSE OF CLASS/UNIT

5. Is the main purpose of the class/unit:

to help pupils with emotional/social problems?   ◯

to give educational help?   ◯

to relieve other classes or schools?   ◯

PREDOMINANT PATTERNS OF BEHAVIOUR

6. We recognise the reluctance of some colleagues to classify children according to their predominant patterns of behaviour but we should be greatly helped by the information. Please give approximate percentage over the Spring Term, 1976. (For this purpose no child should be counted twice.)

[   ]% mainly outgoing, active, aggressive, disruptive, quarrelsome, etc.

☐ % mainly inward-looking, passive, anxious, fearful, socially
isolated, etc.

☐ % with some features from each of the above groups; neither
pattern predominant

EDUCATION

7. What percentage of the pupils have

a. ☐ % no special educational problems?

b. ☐ % some retardation in general school work?

c. ☐ % need for remedial help in the basic subjects?

d. ☐ % both b. and c?

☐ 100 % TOTAL

8. How is the teaching organised?
    Tick column (a) for teaching in class/unit
              (b) for teaching in main or parent school, where known

          (a) (b)
    1.   ◯   ◯ *No specialisation*
    2.   ◯   ◯ *Some specialisation*
    3.   ◯   ◯ *Largely specialisation*
    1.   ◯   ◯ *Some team teaching*
    2.   ◯   ◯ *No team teaching*
    3.   ◯   ◯ *Mostly team teaching*
    1.   ◯   ◯ *Mainly individual teaching*
    2.   ◯   ◯ *A combination of group/individual work*
    3.   ◯   ◯ *Mainly class teaching*

9. Which of the subjects below are taught?
    Tick column (a) if the subject is taught in the class/unit
              (b) if the subject is taught in main or parent school,
                  where known

	(a)	(b)			(a)	(b)	
1.	O	O	English language	11.	O	O	Music
2.	O	O	English literature	12.	O	O	Arts and crafts
3.	O	O	Maths	13.	O	O	Drama and movement
4.	O	O	Geography	14.	O	O	Domestic subjects
5.	O	O	History	15.	O	O	P.E. & allied activities
6.	O	O	Science	16.	O	O	Careers
7.	O	O	Religious or moral education	17.	O	O	Preparation for parenthood
8.	O	O	Modern languages	18.	O	O	Environmental studies
9.	O	O	Technical drawing	19.	O	O	Commercial subjects
10.	O	O	Woodwork and or metal work	20.	O	O	Health education including sex education

Other subjects taught: indicate whether (a) or (b)

		Yes	No
10.	Is remedial teaching part of the normal classroom work at the class/unit?	O	O
	Is remedial teaching a specialist provision		
	within main school?	O	O
	within class/unit?	O	O
	If remedial teaching is a specialist provision within the main school, is it available and used by pupils attending the class/unit?		
	available	O	O
	used	O	O

11. Please name any educational activities, methods, or materials that you have found to be particularly useful within the class/unit.

ASSESSMENT

12. Which people are involved and which tests are used at the different stages in assessment of pupils assigned to the class/unit?

	For selection	During stay	For re-entry
People: *Head of school*	○	○	○
Class teacher	○	○	○
Teacher i/c unit	○	○	○
School counsellor	○	○	○
Pastoral care staff	○	○	○
Psychologist	○	○	○
Social worker	○	○	○
Others—please specify below	○	○	○
Tests: *Standard I.Q. tests*	○	○	○
Standard attainment tests in basic subjects	○	○	○
Others—please specify below	○	○	○

People:

Tests:

13. What has been

the shortest duration of attendance for a given pupil?

the longest duration of attendance for a given pupil?

the most usual duration of attendance for most pupils?

At time of admittance, is duration of attendance

   ◯   planned?   ◯   unplanned?

SUPPORTING AGENCIES

14. Who is available to support and advise the teacher
     (a) within the school?

    (b) outside the school?

15. What special problems have been encountered in the functioning
     of the class/unit?

16. In what ways does the provision within the class/unit differ from that
     to which the pupils have been accustomed in their parent school or
     school?

    General approach:

Methods of teaching:

Please use this space for any comments you wish to make, and accept our thanks for your co-operation.

Signed . . . .

Date . . . .

Appendix D
Cluster analysis of treatments

Question 10*—Two methods of analysis to identify possible clusters of treatments according to use were carried out. The first using an elementary linkage analysis yielded no clusters but the second, which was based on Wishart's (1969) clustering by mode analysis using the phi coefficients, yielded four very weak clusters. The threshold used was $r = 0.27$ and the four clusters were:

Cluster 1: treatments 2, 7, 8, 12, 13, 14, 18
Cluster 2: treatments 5, 17, 21
Cluster 3: treatments 9, 10, 15, 16
Cluster 4: treatments 4, 6, 20

with treatments 1, 3, 11, 19 and 22 not belonging clearly to any of these. The figure shows how these clusters combine.

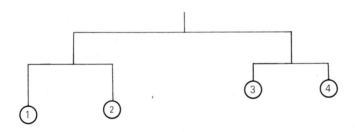

Pattern of clusters identified

* from the main questionnaire (see Appendix B).

Appendix E
Behaviourist and psychodynamic schools

From the twenty-two approaches to treatment given in question 10,* three were selected as being strongly suggestive of an orientation towards behaviourist learning theory (15, 10 and 4) and three as being strongly suggestive of a psychodynamic orientation (9, 16 and 12). If a school indicated that it used two or more of these approaches in any one of these two groups it was withdrawn from the total sample and placed into one of three categories which were labelled, behaviourist schools, dynamic schools and eclectic schools (that is, using two or more in both groups). Sixteen schools were labelled behaviourist, nineteen dynamic and seven eclectic. The behaviourist and dynamic schools were then compared on the major variables and the most notable, and possibly most interesting, findings are given below:

Question	Behaviourist	Dynamic
1—Type of school		
Boarding	5	9
Day	9	5
Mixed day/boarding	2	2
4—Age range of schools		
Senior	4	6
Primary	4	4
All age	7	9
Not specified	1	0
7—Mean percentages of pupils in each of the IQ ranges specified		
Very much below average	5 %	1 %
Below average	26 %	12 %
Average (low)	48 %	41 %
Average (high)	18 %	33 %

* All questions discussed in this Appendix are from the main questionnaire (See Appendix B).

Question	Behaviourist	Dynamic
Above average	2%	11%
Very much above average	1%	2%
8—Mean percentage of pupils in each of the specified levels of achievement in relation to potential on entry		
Not underachieving	7%	4%
Slightly underachieving	25%	21%
Seriously underachieving	39%	49%
Very seriously underachieving	29%	26%
9—Mean percentage of pupils within the disorder categories used		
Conduct disorders	51%	30%
Neurotic disorders	15%	26%
Mixed conduct/neurotic disorders	15%	22%
Developmental disorders	6%	9%
Psychosis	2%	3%
Personality disorders	4%	2%
Educational disorders	3%	4%
Others	0%	1%

The data from questions 10 and 17 clearly underline that we are dealing here with two groups of schools having a leaning towards two particular theoretical viewpoints rather than a wholesale commitment to and practice of those viewpoints. There are, nevertheless, some very interesting and possibly systematic differences between the two groups, particularly when they are seen in reference to the data for the total group of schools for the maladjusted, which are not only suggestive of possible research but almost demand it. A notable example of this (see tabulated responses to question 41) is the challenging finding that the difference between the totals of outcomes by recommendation to ordinary schools or schools other than those for emotional or behavioural difficulties is equivalent to 94% of the difference between the two totals of outcomes.

Question 10 Percentages of schools using a treatment and perceiving a treatment to be effective with particular disorders

Treatment/number	1	2	3	4	5	6	7	8	9	10	11	12	13	14	15	16	17	18	19	20	21	22
Treatments used																						
Behaviourist	81	100	38	88	63	38	100	94	0	88	100	75	94	56	38	0	94	88	88	94	75	81
Dynamic	95	100	11	26	74	37	100	95	90	0	95	95	90	53	0	37	95	100	95	79	95	74
Conduct disorders																						
Behaviourist	25	75	6	44	6	6	31	13	0	38	75	0	19	19	25	6	38	31	19	44	6	69
Dynamic	21	53	0	5	21	0	21	5	5	5	58	16	16	16	0	5	58	26	42	5	37	53
Neurotic disorders																						
Behaviourist	13	88	6	19	6	0	25	38	0	13	63	38	38	38	13	0	31	44	31	25	31	25
Dynamic	5	74	0	0	11	11	16	26	68	0	42	26	37	11	0	11	32	53	37	5	37	11
Mixed conduct/neurotic disorders																						
Behaviourist	25	69	0	25	0	0	25	13	0	19	69	6	38	25	0	0	31	38	19	44	13	38
Dynamic	11	79	0	11	16	0	16	11	37	0	58	26	37	16	0	16	26	37	37	5	37	53
All disorders																						
Behaviourist	19	69	6	19	6	0	19	6	0	19	69	19	25	25	13	0	44	19	6	19	0	50
Dynamic	32	58	5	5	16	5	21	16	26	5	58	16	21	5	0	16	26	16	37	0	16	42

Question 11 Importance of features in running a community for disturbed pupils (5 = most important)

	No response	Weightings				
		1	2	3	4	5
Pupil involvement in management						
Behaviourist	13	19	19	44	0	6
Dynamic	5	16	21	26	16	16
Scholastic progress						
Behaviourist	0	6	13	31	50	0
Dynamic	0	0	0	47	32	21
Gaining of insight						
Behaviourist	0	0	13	13	25	50
Dynamic	0	0	5	0	53	42
Accepting relationships						
Behaviourist	6	0	0	0	31	63
Dynamic	0	0	0	5	21	74
Expressive work in the arts						
Behaviourist	13	6	31	31	43	0
Dynamic	5	5	11	58	21	0
Opportunities for regression						
Behaviourist	0	25	19	44	13	0
Dynamic	0	5	37	37	16	5
Routine and discipline						
Behaviourist	0	0	6	19	44	31
Dynamic	0	5	5	47	21	21

Note Figures are in percentages of schools responding

Question 17 Pupils receiving specific medical and psychological treatments (in percentages)

	Behaviourist	Dynamic	Significance
Individual psychotherapy	2	19	$P < 0.003$
Group psychotherapy	0	6	None
Behaviour therapy	18	1	$P = 0.05$
Drug treatment	9	6	None

Question 41   Outcomes for underage leavers (means)

Transfer or other provision		Behaviourist	Dynamic
To other maladjusted schools	by parents	0·1	0·2
	excluded	0·1	0·4
	recommended	2·9	1·8
To other special schools	by parents	0·1	0·3
	excluded	0·2	0·1
	recommended	3·9	0·5
To ordinary schools	by parents	0·6	0·7
	excluded	0·1	0·0
	recommended	6·8	4·1
Otherwise provided for	by parents	0·4	0·2
	excluded	0·1	0·3
	recommended	0·6	0·8
	TOTALS	15·9	9·4

References

Barker, P. (1974). *The Residential Psychiatric Treatment of Children*. Crosby Lockwood Staples.

Bridgeland, M. (1971). *Pioneer work with Maladjusted Children: a Study in the Development of Therapeutic Education*. Staples Press.

Davie, R. (1968). 'The behaviour and adjustment of seven-year-old children: some results from the National Child Development Study (1958 cohort)' *British Journal of Educational Psychology*, **38**, 1–2.

Department of Education and Science (1973). *Statistics of Education, 1972*, vol. 1, *Schools*. HMSO.

Laslett, R. (1977). *Educating Maladjusted Children*. Crosby Lockwood Staples.

Ministry of Education (1945). *Handicapped Pupils and Schools Health Service Regulations*. HMSO.

Ministry of Education (1955). *Report of the Committee on Maladjusted Children* (Underwood Report). HMSO.

Nie, N. H. et al. (1970). *Statistical Package for the Social Sciences*. New York: McGraw-Hill.

Rutter, M. (1975). *Helping Troubled Children*. Penguin.

Rutter, M., Tizard, J. and Whitmore, K. (1970). *Education, Health and Behaviour*. Longman.

Tait, F. (1973). 'Boarding schools for maladjusted children: a psychiatric viewpoint' *Journal of the Association of Workers with Maladjusted Children*, **3**, 10–19.

West, D. (1967). *The Young Offender*. Duckworth and Penguin.

Williams, N. (1962). 'Criteria for recovery of maladjusted children in residential schools'. M.Ed. thesis, Durham University.

Wilson, M. and Evans, M. (1980). *Education of Disturbed Pupils*, Schools Council Working Paper 65. Evans/Methuen Educational.

Wishart, D. (1969). *Numerical Taxonomy*. Academic Press.

Wolff, S. (1973). *Children Under Stress*. Penguin.

The consultative committee

Chairman

R B Laslett (Chairman) Tutor, Advanced Course for Teachers of Maladjusted Children, University of Birmingham

J. Armstrong Headmaster, Mulberry Bush School, Witney
Helen M. Carter Schools Council
J Chambers Regents Park Secondary School, Southampton
P/Sgt D Coxall Lancashire Constabulary
J R Fish HM Inspector of Schools, Special Education
J Harry Headteacher, Special Unit for Maladjusted Pupils, Pembroke Teachers' Centre, Dyfed
Mrs S Jacobs Senior Lecturer in Applied Social Studies, Hatfield Polytechnic
N Jones Principal Educational Psychologist, Oxford LEA
Mrs P Jones Education Officer, National Union of Teachers
M Mahoney Manningham Middle School, Leeds
C Mowforth Remedial teacher, Berkshire
M Pickles Bracken Bank Primary School, Keighley
A M S Poole Headmaster, Eastfield School, Wolverhampton
Miss S Roberts School Counsellor, Holland Park School, London W8
Prof M Rutter Department of Child Psychiatry, Institute of Psychiatry, London
Dr Mary Shaw School Medical Officer
A F Smithies Thomas Beckett RC Upper School, Northampton
Murray Ward Schools Council
Miss C Whitehead Social Services Department, Wandsworth, London SW18
Norman Williams Schools Council
Mrs S A Williams Headmistress, Colebrooke School, London N1

Project team

Dr Mary Wilson, OBE ⎱
Mrs Mary Evans   ⎰ Joint Directors
Jennifer Kiek Research officer
R L Dawson Research officer